Diving & Snorkeling

Southern California
& the Channel Islands

David Krival

LONELY PLANET PUBLICATIONS
Melbourne • Oakland • London • Paris

Diving & Snorkeling Southern California
   & the Channel Islands
- A Lonely Planet Pisces Book

1st Edition – June 2001

Published by
Lonely Planet Publications
90 Maribyrnong St., Footscray, Victoria 3011, Australia

Other offices
150 Linden Street, Oakland, California 94607, USA
10a Spring Place, London NW5 3BH, UK
1 rue du Dahomey, 75011 Paris, France

Photographs
by photographers as indicated

Front cover photograph, by Kathy deWet-Oleson
Underwater photographer meets giant black sea bass

Back cover photographs
Spotted triopna nudibranch, by Bonnie Cardone
Garibaldi, California's state fish, by David McCray
Elephant seals and sea lions on San Miguel Island,
   by Andrew Sallmon

The images in this guide are available for licensing
   from Lonely Planet Images
email: lpi@lonelyplanet.com.au

ISBN 1 86450 293 2

Although the author
and publisher have tried
to make the information
as accurate as possible,
they accept no responsi-
bility for any loss, injury
or inconvenience sus-
tained by any person
using this book.

Contents

North Channel Shore Dive Sites   76

Santa Catalina Island Dive Sites   83

San Clemente Island Dive Sites   94

Santa Barbara Island Dive Sites   101

San Nicolas Island Dive Sites   106

Author

David Krival

David had his first scuba experience in a flooded limestone quarry in
Wisconsin in 1975. After moving to Southern California in 1978, he
developed an intense fascination with the marine environment. A free-
diver and a scuba diver, he has explored all of the Channel Islands, as
well as Cortes and Tanner Banks. He has also dived extensively on Baja
California's Pacific Coast and in the Sea of Cortez. He's been a divemaster since 1993.

A former amateur baseball player, he has been the full-time editor
of *HardBall, America's Adult Baseball Magazine* since 1990. In the mid-90s, he began writing occasional articles for diving magazines.

Contributing Photographers

Bonnie Cardone, who contributed the majority of images for this
book, became a certified diver in 1973 and worked for *Skin Diver
Magazine* from 1976 to 1999. During her 23 years there, more than 900
of her articles and thousands of her photos were published in the magazine. In January 1999, Bonnie was named Woman Diver of the Year
by the Women's Scuba Association, and was inducted into its Women
Divers Hall of Fame in 2000. Bonnie is co-author of *Shipwrecks of
Southern California* (1989) and *Fireside Diver* (1992). She is now a full-
time freelance writer and photographer.

Photographers Kathy deWet-Oleson, David McCray and Andrew Sallmon also contributed many
unique and valuable images.

From the Author

To put this book together, I drew on the skills, knowledge and experience of many people. Author-
photographer Bonnie Cardone supplied most of the images and wrote the section on underwater
photography. Marine researcher and photographer Kathy deWet-Olsen provided rare images and wrote
the giant sea bass sidebar. Ecologist Michael Graham consulted on a variety of scientific matters.

Captain Eric and Admiral Cyndie Bowman of the dive boat *Peace* helped me with the navigational charts and provided invaluable moral support. Patient and tolerant Lonely Planet editors Roslyn
Bullas and Sarah Jane Hubbard kept me more or less on schedule.

I am also grateful to my adventurous friends for sharing their passion for diving in the miracu-
lous waters of Southern California: Chip Bissell, Bob McClurg, Fidel Luna, Roland Hermann, George
Williams, Warren Yeager, Beth Tom, Larry Dimatteo and Bob Kieran.

Finally, without the use of authoritative reference works, a project like this would be nearly impos-
sible. A partial list: *Diving Pioneers, An Oral History of Diving in America* by Eric Hanauer; *20,000 Jobs
Under the Sea, The History of Diving and Underwater Engineering* by Torrance Parker; *Pacific Coast
Inshore Fishes* by Daniel Gottshall; *Pacific Coast Subtidal Marine Invertebrates: A Fishwatcher's Guide* by
Daniel Gottshall & Laurence Laurent; *Probably More Than You Want to Know About the Fishes of the
Pacific Coast* by Robin Milton Love; *Marine Mammals of California* by Robert T. Orr & Roger C. Helm;
Shipwrecks of Southern California by Bonnie J. Cardone & Patrick Smith; *Southern California's Best
Beach Dives* by Dale & Kim Sheckler.

From the Publisher

This first edition was produced in Lonely Planet's U.S. office under direction from Roslyn Bullas, the Pisces Books publishing manager. Sarah Jane Hubbard edited the text and photos, with invaluable contributions from David Lauterborn and Erin Corrigan. Emily Douglas designed the book's content and cover. Colin Bishop, Brad Lodge, Sara Nelson, John Spelman and Eric Thomsen created the maps under the supervision of U.S. cartography manager Alex Guilbert. Lindsay Brown reviewed the Marine Life sections for scientific accuracy.

Pisces Pre-Dive Safety Guidelines

Before embarking on a scuba diving, skin diving or snorkeling trip, carefully consider the following to help ensure a safe and enjoyable experience:

- Possess a current diving certification card from a recognized scuba diving instructional agency (if scuba diving)
- Be sure you are healthy and feel comfortable diving
- Obtain reliable information about physical and environmental conditions at the dive site (e.g., from a reputable local dive operation)
- Be aware of local laws, regulations and etiquette about marine life and environment
- Dive at sites within your experience level; if possible, engage the services of a competent, professionally trained dive instructor or divemaster

Underwater conditions vary significantly from one region, or even site, to another. Seasonal changes can significantly alter site and dive conditions. These differences influence the way divers dress for a dive and what diving techniques they use.

There are special requirements for diving in any area, regardless of location. Before your dive, ask about environmental characteristics that can affect your diving and how trained local divers deal with these considerations.

Warning & Request

Things change—dive site conditions, regulations, topside information. Nothing stays the same for long. Your feedback on this book will be used to help update and improve the next edition. Excerpts from your correspondence may appear in *Planet Talk,* our quarterly newsletter, or *Comet,* our monthly email newsletter. Please let us know if you do not want your letter published or your name acknowledged.

Correspondence can be addressed to:
Lonely Planet Publications
Pisces Books
150 Linden Street
Oakland, CA 94607
email: pisces@lonelyplanet.com

Introduction

Abundant, colorful marine life, a large fleet of professional dive charter boats and year-round temperate weather make Southern California one of the world's great diving destinations. Although diving conditions are more challenging than typical tropical conditions, correctly equipped and prepared divers at every level of skill and experience can enjoy a wide variety of world-class sites in Southern California waters.

On sheltered, shallow to medium-depth inshore reefs along the Southern California coast and around the Channel Islands, less experienced divers may safely explore a unique and beautiful environment, the giant kelp forest. While weaving through the kelp stands, divers may encounter 50 species of fish and invertebrates in a matter of minutes. Lobsters and moray eels peek out from their hiding places beneath sponge-covered rocks. Male sheephead and golden garibaldi patrol their territories along the reef. It is not uncommon for divers to be accompanied by a curious harbor seal or a playful sea lion while cruising through the kelp.

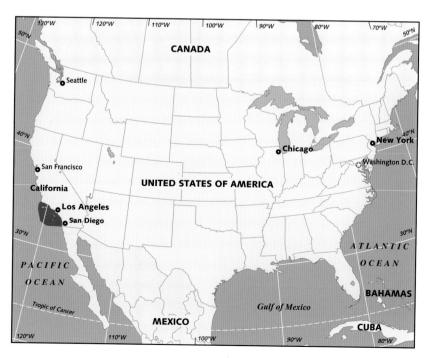

In quiet, sunlit coves, whether you're snorkeling or on scuba, you can find halibut and angel sharks half-buried in the sand, squadrons of bat rays flying in formation and shimmering schools of baitfish and mackerel swirling in mid-water.

For advanced divers few diving experiences compare to the thrill of descending the anchor line toward an unseen offshore seamount. As the plankton bloom clears below the thermocline, you'll find yourself immersed in silence, approaching the face of a sheer wall 100ft (30m) below the surface, 100ft (30m) above the bottom. As your eyes adjust to the soft light, you'll see that the rock is alive—covered with anemones, scallops, cup corals, brittle stars and tube worms. Octopuses and tiny fish hide in the nooks and crannies, while schools of rockfish hover overhead.

Although there are many noteworthy mainland beach sites, most of the best dive sites in Southern California are miles off the mainland, around the Channel Islands. With the exception of a few sites on Catalina, these sites are only accessible by boat. Unlike many tropical dive-charter operators, Southern California dive boats rarely provide in-water divemasters or tour guides. If you are travelling alone the boat operator may try to match you with a more experienced buddy, but it isn't always possible.

This guide contains detailed information on 60 great sites: how to get there, skill level, topography, typical conditions, marine life and photographic subjects. Some sites will challenge the skills of advanced recreational divers; others were chosen because they are suitable for novices or divers with little experience in Southern California waters. Suggestions in the Diving Health & Safety and Diving in Southern California sections will help you prepare for an enjoyable diving trip. Other sections of this book provide information on local climate, history, geology and outdoor activities, to help you make the most of your time in Southern California, both above water and below.

BONNIE CARDONE

Point Dume State Park, here seen from the air, offers visitors the chance to hike within an ancient coastal bluff sand dune ecosystem.

Overview

KATHY DEWET-OLESON

Southern California's scalloped coastline runs more or less northwest to southeast from Point Conception to the border of Mexico, partially sheltering the waters of the Southern California Bight from Pacific storms. The inner waters of the bight are known, from north to south, as the Santa Barbara Channel, the San Pedro Channel and the Gulf of Santa Catalina.

Across the Santa Barbara Channel, a chain of four islands (Anacapa, Santa Cruz, Santa Rosa and San Miguel) faces the mainland coast from Ventura to Point Conception. These are the North Channel Islands. Four more islands (Santa Catalina, Santa Barbara, San Nicolas and San Clemente) form the South Channel Islands, scattered from 25 to 65 miles (40 to 105km) south and southwest of Santa Monica Bay. In all cases, the island shore that faces the nearest mainland coast is called the front side. The side that faces the open ocean is called the back side.

Geology

Some people fret that Southern California might someday fall into the sea. In some respects, it already has. Forty million years ago the coastline ran south from Point Conception, not southeast as it does today. The Southern California Bight and the Channel Islands didn't exist.

Just offshore, a huge portion of the earth's crust called the Farallon Plate had been moving east, colliding with and sliding under the North American Plate for millions of years. This process, called subduction, created an oceanic trench and a coastal mountain range. The ancient trench is still there, running north-south about a hundred miles offshore, but nearly everything just east of it has changed.

About 40 million years ago subduction ceased in Southern California as the Farallon Plate slipped completely under the North American Plate. This brought the North American Plate into contact with the Pacific Plate. Subsequently, the region south of Point Conception became a complex strike-slip fault zone. A slip fault occurs when colliding plates grind and move horizontally relative to each other. Slip fault systems can drastically rearrange the landscape in relatively short periods of geologic time. Although the San Andreas is the primary fault in Southern California, there are hundreds of minor ones where the crust has buckled under the stress of enormous forces.

When the Pacific and North American Plates collided, a piece of the coastal mountain range, which was separated from an inland range by an arm of the

11

Great Valley, began to wheel around 90° clockwise, pushing the valley and inland mountains before it. The inland mountains had been east of the coastal range; today they lie to the south. The valley is now the Santa Barbara Channel. The inland mountains became the North Channel Islands.

About 18,000 years ago, during the last Ice Age, sea levels fell about 400ft (120m), and the North Channel Island chain became a single land mass, since called Santa Rosae Island. As the ice receded and sea levels rose, the saddles between Santa Rosae's peaks filled with water, forming San Miguel, Santa Rosa, Santa Cruz and Anacapa Islands.

Farther south a complex series of collisions and slippages displaced coastal mountains and inland valleys from their original positions east of the subduction trench. Some of the valleys became the San Pedro Channel, the Outer Santa Barbara Passage and the Gulf of Catalina. Surrounded by water, mountains became San Nicolas Island, Santa Barbara Island, Santa Catalina Island, San Clemente Island, Tanner Bank and Cortes Bank.

The erosive action of wind and waves has also reshaped the coast and the islands. On the back side of San Clemente Island and the ocean side of the Palos Verdes Peninsula, natural terraces cut into the hillsides give dramatic evidence of this. Each terrace, some now a few hundred feet above sea level, represents an ancient beach.

Santa Cruz Island, like the rest of the Channel Islands, was formed by geologic activity over millions of years.

Geography

Greater Los Angeles is the economic and political hub of Southern California. More than 9 million people live in the 88 incorporated cities of Los Angeles County, but the region of dense population and urban development spills into

Ventura, Orange and Riverside Counties without significant interruption. If it weren't for Camp Pendleton (the large military reserve in San Diego County) and a 10-mile (16km) stretch of mountainous open land between the western San Fernando Valley and the population centers of Ventura County, everything from the Mexican border to Ventura would be a contiguous metropolitan area with more than 20 million inhabitants.

Bounded by mountains on the north and east and the ocean on the south and west, urban Southern California is fascinatingly multiethnic, with large enclaves of recent and not-so-recent immigrants proudly clinging to their cultural and linguistic traditions. Nonetheless, some of Southern California's inland urban sprawl is crowded, smoggy, noisy, dangerous and nondescript. Even with the recent addition of a monorail system, public transportation is not very good. In areas street crime (drugs, gangs and prostitution) is a serious problem.

Along the coast and in the mountains and deserts, life is less vexing. Santa Barbara has a quiet harbor, a lot of bed-and-breakfast hotels, a botanical garden and some interesting Spanish ruins. Ventura's Main Street is a funky mix of trendy restaurants and secondhand stores. Ventura Harbor is the headquarters of Channel Islands National Park. Even gritty Oxnard, with its cargo port, military bases, farms and commercial fishing fleet, has the Channel Islands Marina.

Orange, San Diego and L.A. Counties' beach cities are relatively affluent, but can get crowded, especially in the summer. Traffic can be maddening and parking scarce. Venice is a magnet for eccentrics of every description. Santa Monica Pier, Redondo Pier and Ports of Call (San Pedro) are touristy but fun. The upscale Long Beach waterfront has the Aquarium of the Pacific. Huntington Beach attracts weekenders from Orange, Riverside and San Bernardino Counties. Laguna Beach has a summer arts and crafts festival. Newport Beach is strictly for the rich and nautical. Oceanside is a military town, unlike Del Mar (with its horseracing) and La Jolla (home of the Scripps Institute). San Diego has Mission Bay (with Sea World) and the Navy's mothballed fleet.

History

North America's first human settlers migrated across the Bering Strait from Asia, probably during the last Ice Age. At least 11,000 years ago the Chumash people settled the coastal region from Point Arguello to the Palos Verdes Peninsula and the Channel Islands. Geographically isolated from the warlike peoples of the interior, the Chumash developed a prosperous maritime culture and a peaceful trading relationship with the mainland Gabrieleno people. On San Nicolas Island, the Nicolenos, closely related to the Chumash by language and culture, hunted pinnipeds and fished.

The Portuguese sailor Cabrillo charted the region in the early 1600s, but the Spanish didn't begin to colonize until 1769. The Spanish established a string of missions, towns (pueblos) and forts (presidios) in the region: San Diego (1769), San Gabriel (1771), Los Angeles (1781) and Santa Barbara (1782). By the time

Mexico gained independence from Spain in 1821, Los Angeles had become an important agricultural community, exporting olives, wine, meat, cattle hides and sea otter furs.

In the late 18th century the mainland Chumash and Gabrielenos were herded into the missions, baptized and enslaved by Spanish soldiers and priests. They died of measles, syphilis, malnutrition and abuse. For the most part, their cultures died with them. The island Chumash and Nicolenos lasted into the 19th century, when they were murdered or dispersed by Portuguese, Russian and American seal hunters and whalers, with the enthusiastic assistance of adventurers from many Christian nations. While they were at it, these pilgrims killed all the sea otters, most of the gray whales and all but a handful of the elephant seals between Point Conception and Mexico's Guadalupe Islands.

As early as the 1820s, American traders and settlers had been welcomed by the Mexican governors. In 1845 the United States annexed Texas, which had been an independent republic since 1836 and a province of Mexico before that. Understandably, Mexico broke off relations and ordered all U.S. citizens deported from California.

The Mexican-American War began in Texas in May 1846. Acting without orders, John Fremont, a U.S. Army captain stationed in California to protect U.S. citizens on the overland trails, launched a military campaign in northern California. He captured the town of Sonoma and announced the formation of the California (Bear Flag) Republic in June 1846.

Fremont's independent act of rebellion (or banditry, depending on whose history books you read) forced the U.S. to include California in its military and

A monument to the Portuguese sailor Cabrillo,
who charted the region in the early 1600s, sits atop San Miguel Island.

political agenda. By July the Bear Flag Republic was defunct, and American warships occupied the ports of San Francisco, Monterey and San Diego. On August 13, 1846, Commodore John Stockton and Captain Fremont captured Los Angeles. The U.S. Army, under the command of General Winfield Scott, captured Mexico City in September 1847. According to the terms of the Treaty of Guadalupe Hidalgo, the U.S. paid $15 million for the territory that now encompasses New Mexico, Arizona, Nevada and California.

Driven by the myth of the Seven Cities of Cibola, the Spanish had searched obsessively and ruthlessly for gold throughout their colonial empire. Less than a year after the U.S. acquired California, James Marshall found the precious metal on the American River near Sacramento. Eighty thousand "miner '49ers" sailed around the horn of South America or trudged across the mountains and deserts. In 1850 California became the 31st state.

Agricultural developments, including the introduction of citrus farming, brought new settlers to Los Angeles. Between 1880 and 1900 the population grew from 11,000 to 100,000. The new city needed water to sustain its growing population and agrarian economy. In 1904 a self-educated Irish immigrant engineer named William Mulholland began to build a 250-mile (400km) aqueduct from the Sierra Nevada Mountains to the valleys north of Los Angeles. Completed in 1913, the aqueduct ensured the survival and growth of Los Angeles but ruined the farmers and ranchers of the Owens Valley.

In the 1900s three new industries provided the economic foundation for Southern California's emergence as one of the world's great centers of population and wealth: oil, entertainment and aerospace/defense. But despite its general prosperity, Southern California has never been without social tensions and economic inequity. Whatever their causes, poverty, street crime and gang violence plague many neighborhoods. Since the '60s, people who can afford to have moved away from Los Angeles and the central suburbs to the beach cities, the foothills, the West Valley suburbs, south Orange County or north San Diego County, or to affluent urban enclaves like Beverly Hills and Brentwood.

Diving History

In the late 19th century, Japanese and Chinese free-divers began harvesting abalone in Malibu and Palos Verdes. By the turn of the 20th century, the Japanese abalone divers had adopted surface-supplied commercial diving equipment, variously known as "hard-hat gear" or "standard diving gear."

From 1907 to the time of WWII, Merritt, Chapman & Scott Divers, Marine Salvage & Construction contracted almost all of the standard diving gear jobs in Southern California. Wearing bulky suits, lead boots and metal helmets, commercial hard-hat divers breathed through a rubber air hose connected to a pumping mechanism on the surface. Commercial divers were an elite group numbering only about a dozen in Southern California and less than 100 nationwide.

They worked on the Los Angeles Harbor, numerous piers and pipelines, and in the Long Beach shipyard.

Recreational diving in Southern California began in the 1930s. A decade before Jacques Cousteau and Emile Gagnan built the first scuba equipment, a free-diving club called the San Diego Bottom Scratchers was founded by Glen Orr, Jack Prodanovich and Ben Stone. Prodanovich is credited with inventing the dive mask, dive goggles, the underwater camera housing, the powerhead and the first American speargun.

The Bottom Scratchers, like most of Southern California's diving pioneers, were avid underwater hunters. Times were hard in 1933. People were jobless and hungry. The ocean's bounty seemed inexhaustible. Diving without fins or wetsuits (the Beaver company of La Jolla began selling the first $\frac{1}{8}$ inch (2mm) neoprene wetsuits in 1956), the Bottom Scratchers fed family and friends on lobsters and abalone that they could grab by hand, and fish caught using wooden spears and fishhooks.

By the late '40s there were 8,000 skin divers in Southern California. This first generation of sport divers contributed significantly to the near-extinction of several species of large, slow-moving fish: giant black sea bass, broomtail grouper and sawtail grouper. (Since 1982 all three have been protected by law, but only the black sea bass has made any sort of comeback in California waters.) Nonetheless, most of these early free-divers were appalled at the advent of scuba diving as a popular sport, correctly reckoning that it would lead to massive depletion of inshore fish and invertebrate populations. As early as the 1950s they began lobbying the California Department of Fish and Game to restrict what scuba divers could take. Their arguments had little immediate effect.

In 1948 Rene Bussoz began selling the Cousteau/Gagnan Aqua-Lung in Southern California. In 1953 his firm became U.S. Divers, a leading manufacturer of diving equipment. In the early '50s Bob Lorenz in Venice, Mel Fisher in Torrance and the Meistrell Brothers (Bob and Bill) in Hermosa Beach all opened retail dive shops. The Meistrell's store, Dive N' Surf, now in Redondo Beach, is the oldest continuously operating dive shop on the West Coast. The Meistrells also established Body Glove, one of the largest wetsuit manufacturers.

In 1951 Chuck Blakeslee and Jim Auxier founded *Skin Diver*, the first periodical dedicated exclusively to sport diving. Originally focused primarily on free-diving and spearfishing, *Skin Diver* evolved with the sport, contributing significantly to the growth of the diving industry by emphasizing underwater photography and dive-related travel.

As recreational diving grew, many divers became concerned with the issues of safety and training. In 1954 Al Tillman and lifeguard Bev Morgan introduced the first formal training programs for skin divers and scuba divers. Within a year, instructors were being trained and certified. A three-digit L.A. County certification card identifies its owner as a scuba pioneer. In 1960 Tillman and Neal Hess organized the National Association of Underwater Instructors (NAUI).

In 1954 *Kingdom of the Sea*, television's first underwater documentary series, included a live broadcast of Zale Parry, one the first female divers, descending to a record-setting 209ft (64m) off Catalina Island. With Tillman, Parry organized the first underwater film festival in Los Angeles in 1957. Airing from 1958 to 1961, *Sea Hunt*, produced by Ivan Tors, filmed by Lamar Boren and starring Lloyd Bridges, became America's most popular TV series, inspiring a generation of future divers.

Since the 1950s sport diving has benefited from a steady progression of technical advances. Southern California remains a center of the world sport-diving industry. Every year local instructors certify tens of thousands of new divers. Every weekend, classes of new divers make their first beach dives at Avenue C in Redondo Beach, Leo Carillo State Park and Avalon Underwater Park on Catalina. From Santa Barbara to San Diego, Southern California's fleet of dive charter boats is busy year-round.

Over the years Southern California divers have become increasingly concerned with conservation issues. Since the 1970s the percentage of scuba divers who consider hunting as their primary underwater activity has fallen dramatically, in part because certifying agencies have successfully promoted scuba diving as a mainstream, social outdoor activity. The spearfishing clubs of the 1950s remain, but they are far outnumbered by "social" diving clubs, most of which are associated with a dive retail store and its instructors.

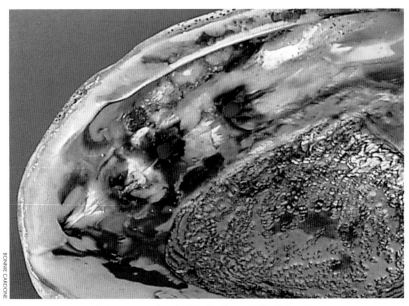

BONNIE CARDONE

Abalone, once abundant in Southern California's waters,
were taken for their delicately flavored flesh and pearlescent shells.

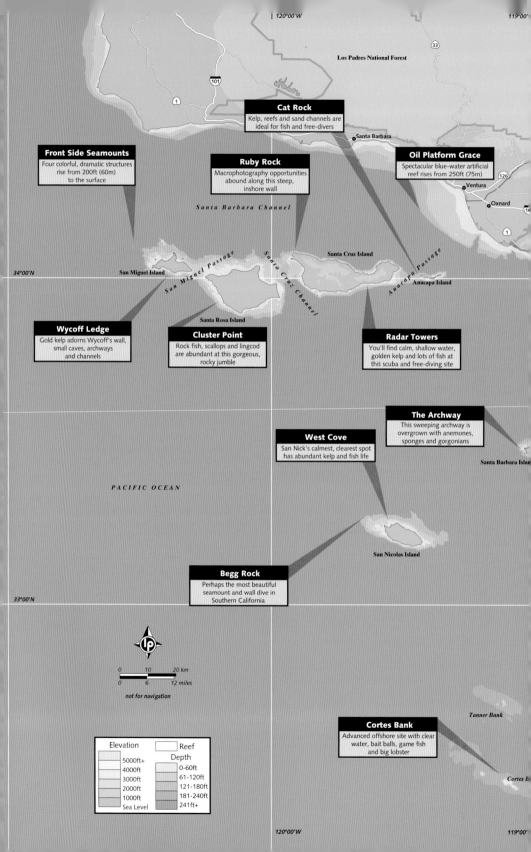

Cat Rock
Kelp, reefs and sand channels are ideal for fish and free-divers

Front Side Seamounts
Four colorful, dramatic structures rise from 200ft (60m) to the surface

Ruby Rock
Macrophotography opportunities abound along this steep, inshore wall

Oil Platform Grace
Spectacular blue-water artificial reef rises from 250ft (75m)

Santa Barbara Channel

Wycoff Ledge
Gold kelp adorns Wycoff's wall, small caves, archways and channels

Cluster Point
Rock fish, scallops and lingcod are abundant at this gorgeous, rocky jumble

Radar Towers
You'll find calm, shallow water, golden kelp and lots of fish at this scuba and free-diving site

The Archway
This sweeping archway is overgrown with anemones, sponges and gorgonians

West Cove
San Nick's calmest, clearest spot has abundant kelp and fish life

Begg Rock
Perhaps the most beautiful seamount and wall dive in Southern California

Cortes Bank
Advanced offshore site with clear water, bait balls, game fish and big lobster

PACIFIC OCEAN

Los Padres National Forest

Santa Barbara
Ventura
Oxnard

San Miguel Passage
San Miguel Island
Santa Cruz Channel
Santa Cruz Island
Anacapa Passage
Anacapa Island
Santa Rosa Island

San Nicolas Island

Santa Barbara Island

Tanner Bank
Cortes B

34°00'N
33°00'N
120°00'W
119°00'

0   10   20 km
0   6   12 miles
not for navigation

Elevation	Reef
5000ft+	Depth
4000ft	0-60ft
3000ft	61-120ft
2000ft	121-180ft
1000ft	181-240ft
Sea Level	241ft+

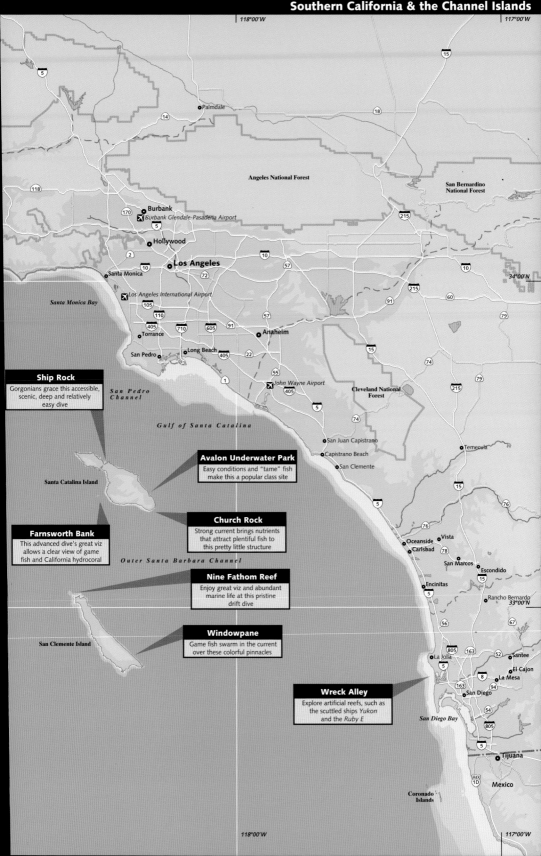

Ship Rock
Gorgonians grace this accessible, scenic, deep and relatively easy dive

Avalon Underwater Park
Easy conditions and "tame" fish make this a popular class site

Church Rock
Strong current brings nutrients that attract plentiful fish to this pretty little structure

Farnsworth Bank
This advanced dive's great viz allows a clear view of game fish and California hydrocoral

Nine Fathom Reef
Enjoy great viz and abundant marine life at this pristine drift dive

Windowpane
Game fish swarm in the current over these colorful pinnacles

Wreck Alley
Explore artificial reefs, such as the scuttled ships *Yukon* and the *Ruby E*

DAVID MCCRAY

Practicalities

Climate

Shielded by the mountains from the surrounding deserts and cooled by the ocean, Southern California has a temperate climate. Summer highs range from 85°F to the low 90s (around 30°C); winter lows are from the mid 50s to the low 60s (13 to 17°C). Except when the Santa Ana winds blow off the high deserts (usually in the fall), offshore breezes keep the beaches 10 to 15°F (6 to 8°C) cooler than the inland areas. Besides heating the air, Santa Ana winds are accompanied by a high pressure system that aggravates Southern California's greatest environmental problem—smog.

Inland Southern California gets about 190 sunny days per year, and the beaches get about 140. Winter is the rainy season, with about 15 inches (38cm) annually.

Water Clarity & Temperature

Many factors influence water clarity and temperature: current, wind, depth and global climatic shifts. Also, inshore and coastal waters are subject to run-off pollution from rainwater and sewers. Generally, the water gets colder as you dive deeper and as you travel farther north or away from the mainland.

By Southern California standards, 30 to 40ft (9 to 12m) of visibility is pretty good. Santa Catalina, San Clemente, Anacapa and Santa Barbara Islands and the Outer Banks are known for good to excellent clarity—50ft is common around Catalina and Clemente, and 100ft is not uncommon at Cortes, Tanner and Farnsworth Banks. Water temperatures generally range from 55 to 65°F (13 to 18°C).

The California Current carries cold water from the Northern Pacific southward along a coastal trench. Where the California Current encounters warm surface water from the Equatorial Pacific, part of it branches off, swirls counterclockwise and heads north, toward the inner islands. This is called the California Countercurrent or the Southern California Eddy. Eventually, the California Countercurrent cools and dissipates, but not before it warms San Clemente, Santa Catalina and to a lesser degree Anacapa and Santa Cruz Islands. As a result, the outer North Channel Islands can be as much as 10°F (6°C) cooler than the inner islands.

Santa Ana winds often move large volumes of surface water, which is then replaced by cold-water upwellings that cause offshore water temperatures to plummet. Cold-water upwellings usually bring nutrients to the upper water column. When exposed to sunlight, these nutrients trigger a burst of planktonic growth called a plankton bloom.

If the current is not strong enough to sweep the plankton away faster than it multiplies, the water column above the thermocline (the horizontal boundary between a warmer upper layer and colder water below) becomes a kind of living soup. This is especially noticeable in summer and in calm sheltered areas around structures. The bloom may be quite thick at the surface, but dramatically thinner below the thermocline.

In the winter the absence of a dramatic thermocline often allows for a thorough mixing of surface and bottom water, which helps dissipate the plankton and other particles suspended in the water column.

BONNIE CARDONE

Kelp thrives in the cool waters of the Channel Islands.

El Niño & La Niña

Every few years a large body of warm water forms in the Central Pacific, then streams northeast toward California's coast. This condition, called El Niño, disrupts global weather patterns on a massive scale. In western North America, El Niño summers tend to be abnormally hot and dry, raising water temperatures off Southern California to 80°F (27°C) in some places. During El Niño winters the Pacific remains abnormally warm.

During El Niño years subtropical species of fish and invertebrates ride the warm currents into Southern California waters. Divers may encounter exotic critters like triggerfish, leopard grouper and pargo. Sea turtles graze on subtropical jellyfish off San Miguel. Tuna and dorado also may come farther north than usual and stay longer. Even bull sharks have been seen in the region.

Many temperate fish and invertebrate species suffer during an El Niño, as do the animals that feed upon them. In some areas the water becomes too warm for kelp to grow, and the local kelp forest ecosystem may disappear. Kelp forests that survive the summer heat may be torn apart by winter storms.

After a year or so the warm water in the Central Pacific disperses, often replaced by a large body of colder-than-normal water called La Niña. Following conditions that were too warm for some local species, abnormally cold water temperatures kill off others (larval lobsters, for example).

Getting There

Los Angeles International Airport (LAX), served by all major airlines, is the port of entry for almost all international travelers flying into Southern California. San Diego is also a port of entry with U.S. Customs and Immigration personnel, but only a handful of international flights arrive there. Burbank, Orange County and San Diego airports serve as regional hubs for western U.S. airlines.

Getting Around

Since public transportation is not very good and you're probably carrying a lot of gear, you'll probably want to drive to the dive sites or dive charter boats. Several companies offer rental cars at competitive rates near each of the region's airports. Thomas Guide map books are an extremely useful tool to help you find your way around. Even the natives feel lost without one. You'll find these regional guides at LAX (at newsstands) and at grocery stores and gas stations throughout Southern California.

Shore diving sites are typically accessed from public beaches along Highways 1 (often called Pacific Coast Highway, or PCH) and 101. Detailed directions to these sites are included in the shore dive site descriptions.

Most of the best dive charter boats are based in five major harbors and marinas—Santa Barbara, Ventura, 22nd Street Landing in San Pedro, Long Beach and San Diego's Mission Bay. The easiest place to catch the Catalina Express is Ports of Call, San Pedro. Though most dive boats provide local and harbor maps upon request, it's helpful to know how to get from LAX to the boat ahead of time.

LAX to Ventura Harbor: Exit LAX on Sepulveda southbound. Get on Hwy 105 east. Within a mile or so, merge onto Hwy 405 north and continue on it for about 10 miles (16km). Just over the top of the hill, get onto Hwy 101 west (toward Ventura) and continue on it for about 30 miles (50km). Exit at Victoria St., turn left (south) and go under the bridge. Take Victoria to Olivas Park Dr. Turn right (west) and take Olivas Park Dr. until it meets Harbor Blvd. Cross Harbor (Olivas becomes Spinnaker at this point). You're in Ventura Harbor. The dive boats are near Hornblower's and Andria's restaurants.

LAX to Santa Barbara Harbor: Follow above directions, but continue on Hwy 101 for 50 miles (80km), until you reach the Cabrillo St. exit in Santa Barbara. This is a left-lane exit. Turn left onto Cabrillo, then left again onto Harbor Way. The entrance to the parking lot is near the north end of the harbor.

LAX to 22nd Street Landing, San Pedro: Exit LAX on Sepulveda southbound. Get on Hwy 105 east, then merge onto Hwy 405 south. After 5 or 6 miles (8 to 10km), take Hwy 110 south to San Pedro. Hwy 110 terminates at Gaffey St., San Pedro. Continue south on Gaffey (no need to turn) until you reach 22nd St. Turn left, cross Pacific Ave. The marina is on your right. You can unload your gear in the short-term parking area near the boats, but you'll have to park across the street in the overnight lot.

LAX to Ports of Call, San Pedro: Follow directions for 22nd Street Landing, only take the Harbor Blvd./Ports of Call exit off Hwy 110, then follow the signs to Ports of Call. Again, you can unload near the landing, but overnight parking is about half a block away.

LAX to Long Beach Harbor: Exit LAX on Sepulveda southbound. Get on Hwy 105 east, then merge onto Hwy 405 south. Take Hwy 405 south to Hwy 710 south. Exit at Pico Ave. Turn right at the end of the off-ramp onto Ocean Blvd., continue to the Long Beach Sportfishing Boat Landing. Unload in short-term parking lot. Park in Sportfishing parking lot.

LAX to Mission Bay, San Diego: Exit LAX on Sepulveda southbound. Get on Hwy 105 east, then merge onto Hwy 405 south. Hwy 405 merges with I-5 in Orange County. Stay on I-5 all the way to San Diego—more than 100 miles (160km) in all. Exit at Sea World Dr. westbound. Turn right onto West Mission Bay Dr., then left on Quivera St. The dive boats are in Quivera Basin.

Time

California is on Pacific Standard Time and, like most of the U.S., observes daylight saving time. When it is noon in California, it is 3pm in New York, 8pm in London and 7am the following day in Sydney.

What to Bring

General Supplies

With the exception of a few relatively isolated shore sites, general supplies are readily at hand throughout Southern California. For shore dives, pack a tarp (to keep the sand off your gear), fresh water (for yourself and to rinse your gear), towels, some snacks, perhaps a first-aid kit (if there's no lifeguard tower nearby), a save-a-dive kit and, if the site is in a city, a pile of quarters to feed the parking meter.

Even in the summer it can be chilly and damp at night—bring a warm sweater or jacket. On a windy outer-island boat trip, an effective windbreaker can make the difference between comfort and borderline hypothermia.

Dive-Related Equipment

You need a 7mm wetsuit or a drysuit to dive comfortably in Southern California. Wetsuit rentals are available at dozens of dive retailers, but drysuit rentals are rare. No matter where you stay or where you plan to go, there will be a dive retailer nearby. Many boat operators will suggest a convenient shop for you or even arrange for rental gear to be delivered to the boat. You can easily rent or buy just about anything you need: BC, regulator, gauges, computers, cameras, safety flares, inflatables, kayaks, etc. The supply of rental gear is plentiful, but not infinite, and a lot of it is reserved for classes; it's a good idea to reserve your gear a week or two in advance, especially in the summer or if you wear an uncommon wetsuit size.

Some boats provide tanks and weight belts. Many dive shops and some boats offer enriched air, if you have a nitrox C-card. Most boats carry spare gear and parts, but you're better off if you bring your own save-a-dive kit (see the Diving Health & Safety section for suggested contents).

If you plan to take game of any kind, you must have a current California fishing license with an Ocean Enhancement Stamp. You can purchase one at any bait shop, most dive retailers and a few other places such as pharmacies and liquor stores. Ask if the boat has live game wells and if you may bring a cooler for game.

Underwater Photography in Southern California

Underwater photography is a popular hobby in Southern California. Most retail dive shops sell (and some rent) underwater cameras and photographic equipment. Professional film and developing services are plentiful.

If you can take underwater photographs in California waters, you can take them anywhere. Photographers here have to deal with challenging conditions that don't exist in tropical destinations. The following are a few of the ones you are likely to come across, along with some suggestions for overcoming them:

Poor visibility Sometimes the waters turn emerald green with plankton; sometimes wind and waves reduce visibility to inches. The solution? Take close-ups. California waters are rich with macro subjects, even in sandy areas.

Surge The bigger the swells on the surface, the deeper the surge. You can't fight surge, but you can use it to carry you hither and yon. Here's how: As the surge carries you forward, look for a subject; as it carries you backward, prepare to shoot. When the surge carries you forward again there will be a momentary lull at the end of the cycle when you'll stay in one place. During this lull, take your picture. Then, as the surge carries you backward, get ready for the next shot. If you want to stay in one place for a couple of shots, find a rock to wrap your legs around (first make sure it has no sea urchins on it).

Low light levels California waters are not as clear as tropical waters. Thus, even when the water looks bright, not as much light is penetrating as you may think. This will become evident when you get your film processed and your photos look as if they were shot at night. The solution? Always use a strobe. A slower shutter speed will help, too—1/30th of a second lets in twice as much light as 1/60th and will brighten your background.

Kelp This fast-growing marine alga creates certain problems. The kelp canopy reduces light underwater, and there are those pesky stipes that wrap around camera parts. The solution? If you want to shoot under the canopy, stay as high in the water as you can so you get the most light possible. If you're on the bottom, shoot using upward angles. Strategically incorporate the sun and light filtering down through the kelp into your composition. A silhouetted diver adds perspective and interest.

Though you can't always prevent kelp from snagging camera parts, you can minimize it by folding strobe arms into a compact package and holding the camera close to your body. If a stipe snags you, gently pull it off or bend the stipe to break it.

—*Bonnie J. Cardone*

Accommodations

Southern California has plentiful accommodations, ranging from four-star hotel suites to low-budget motel rooms. Local chambers of commerce provide excellent information in this regard (see Listings). Rates tend to rise in summer and as you get closer to the beach. Rooms may be scarce on holidays and summer weekends.

Harbor and marina districts can be charming (Santa Barbara), touristy (Long Beach), somewhat isolated (Ventura) or a little grimy (San Pedro). Just about everywhere, however, you'll find plenty of "mainstream" hotels with reasonable prices. On Catalina Island, several hotels cater to divers by offering package deals (see the Activities & Attractions and Listings sections).

Throughout Southern California, state parks and beaches provide public access to primitive and developed campgrounds (see Listings). However, to camp at popular sites you may need to reserve months in advance.

Dining & Food

Southern California's multiculturalism makes it easy to find just about any kind of food you like in or near most harbors: Thai, Chinese, Japanese, Vietnamese, Peruvian, Mexican, Italian, Greek, Moroccan and fresh seafood to name just a few.

The evening before a dive trip (most overnight trips leave around midnight), many Southern California divers like to stow their gear aboard then catch a meal in one of the restaurants overlooking the moorings. If you do likewise, you may meet some of your companions on the trip. Marinas are full of people who live and work on boats, so with few exceptions the dress code at even the best harbor restaurants is very informal, and the prices are reasonable.

What's for Dinner?

Increased consumer demand and poor fishing practices are detrimental to the populations of many fish species worldwide. The choices you make when buying seafood at local restaurants and stores can have an impact on the species' survival. The following species have been overfished and their populations drastically reduced. You can avoid contributing to their decline by not purchasing them.

Bluefin tuna	Shark (any kind)
Lingcod	Sheephead
Rockfish/Pacific red snapper/rock cod	Swordfish
Sablefish/butterfish/black cod	Any fish caught by the live-trapping method
Salmon (farmed)	

For more information about selecting seafood, contact the Audubon Living Oceans Program (which publishes the *Audubon Seafood Lover's Almanac*) at www .audubon.org. The Monterey Bay Aquarium offers its *Seafood Watch* chart at www.montereybayaquarium.com.

KATHY DEWET-OLESON

Activities & Attractions

Southern California's marinas, beaches, state parks and national parks provide regulated public access to marine and outdoor recreational activities, such as camping, surfing, fishing, tide pooling, kayaking, hiking, caving, archaeology and whale watching. There are four marine-mammal care centers in the region and a huge state-of-the-art aquarium. Santa Catalina Island has been Southern California's marine playground for generations.

State Parks & Beaches

Although each facility within the California park system is unique, they fall into six basic categories: **state parks** (large areas of scenic, scientific, natural or cultural value, managed for both recreation and preservation); **state historic parks** (structures and lands of historic interest); **state wilderness** (areas managed to preserve the primeval character of the land, no permanent structures permitted); **state reserves** (areas with protected flora, fauna and geology); and **state recreation areas** and **state beaches** (both are areas that provide public outdoor recreation to large numbers of visitors).

The park system publishes lots of useful maps, guidebooks and pamphlets, including *Day Hiker's Guide to California's State Parks* and *Dive In! to a California State Park*. For general park information, log on to www.cal-parks.ca.gov. To reserve a campsite, access www.reserveamerica.com. To request printed materials or reserve a campsite, call ☎ 800-444-7275.

Channel Islands National Park

Channel Islands National Park consists of the four North Channel Islands—Anacapa, Santa Cruz, Santa Rosa and San Miguel—and Santa Barbara Island (about 40 miles (65km) due south of the northern chain). The boundaries of the park extend 1 mile (1.6km) into the waters around each island. The Channel Islands National Marine Sanctuary extends 6 miles (9.6km) from each shoreline.

Among the least visited of the national parks, Channel Islands National Park is almost completely wild—worth seeing even if you never dive there. There are extensive sea caves and huge seabird colonies on Santa Cruz and Anacapa. Santa Cruz is also a fascinating paleontological and archaeological site, with pygmy mammal fossils and some of the oldest human artifacts in North America. San

Miguel is home to six species of pinnipeds: northern elephant seals, sea lions, northern fur seals, California sea lions, harbor seals and Steller sea lions. Santa Rosa has groves of rare Torrey pine, as well as island foxes, elk and deer. Santa Barbara Island has one of the largest sea lion rookeries in the world, as well as an elephant seal colony.

Although public and private diving and fishing boats frequent the waters around them, the islands themselves are not easily accessible to the public. There are no stores or restaurants and most of the campsites are primitive. On some islands you have to carry in fresh water.

Camping—even setting foot—on the islands is strictly controlled by the National Park Service, the Channel Island National Marine Sanctuary, the Channel Island Nature Conservancy (a nongovernmental group) and their three concessionaires, **Island Packers** in Ventura Harbor and Oxnard's Channel Islands Marina (☎ 805-642-1393 and 805-382-1779, respectively; www.islandpackers.com), **Truth Aquatics** (☎ 805-962-1127, www.truthaquatics.com) in Santa Barbara Harbor and **Channel Islands Aviation** (☎ 805-987-1301, www.flycia.com) at Camarillo Airport.

Whale Watching & Other Harbor Activities

In Southern California, whale watching is big business and is hugely popular with the public. From December through March, when gray whales migrate from Alaska to Mexico, whale-watching tour boats operate out of every major harbor and marina from Santa Barbara to San Diego.

KATHY DEWET-OLESON

California whale watchers can get up-close and personal views of
gray, blue and humpback whales.

In L.A. County, many boats run several trips per day out of King Harbor in Redondo Beach, as well as San Pedro's Ports of Call and 22nd Street Landing. In summer, when the blues and humpbacks feed on krill in the Santa Barbara Channel, you can see them from boats out of Ventura, Oxnard and Santa Barbara.

Besides whale watching, Southern California's harbors and marinas offer a wide variety of enjoyable activities: kayak, paddleboat and sailboat rentals, dining, harbor tours, fishing charters and sailing lessons. For more information, to make reservations or to get directions, see the Listings section in this book or simply search in the yellow pages of the phone book under Marinas, Boat Rentals or Fishing Parties.

DAVID MCCRAY

Visitors to MMCC can view pinnipeds up-close.

The Marine Mammal Care Center (MMCC)

Established in 1987 as part of the federally mandated marine mammal stranding network, the Marine Mammal Care Center (at Fort MacArthur, 3601 S. Gaffey St., San Pedro, ☎ 310-548-5677, www.mar3ine.org) treats more than 200 pinnipeds every year, mainly California sea lions, northern elephant seals and harbor seals, as well as a few northern fur seals and Steller sea lions. Similar facilities operate in Laguna Beach, Santa Barbara and San Diego.

The center is open to the public. Admission is free, though donations are accepted. Docents guide tours on weekends and holidays. Separated from the critters by a walkway and a chain-link fence, visitors can watch feedings and treatments, and learn to identify pinnipeds at fairly close quarters. The center has a small full-time professional staff and is supported by its volunteers and their non-profit organization, Mar³ine.

The Aquarium of the Pacific

Dedicated to the study and preservation of the marine environment, the Aquarium of the Pacific (100 Aquarium Way, Long Beach, ☎ 562-590-3100, www .aquariumofpacific.org) opened in 1998. Its 50 exhibit tanks, ranging from 5,000 to 350,000 gallons (19,000 to 1,325,000 liters), provide living space for 10,000 animals representing 550 species in three habitat zones (Northern Pacific, Southern California/Baja and Tropical Pacific). Their website has useful maps, exhibit updates and information about nearby attractions.

Santa Catalina Island

Everybody loves Santa Catalina, the only Channel Island not controlled by the National Park Service or the U.S. Navy. Half a century ago David Niven and Errol Flynn made a Friday habit of racing their sports cars from the Paramount lot to Marina Del Rey. There they would jump on Flynn's yacht and sail to Avalon to fish for yellowtail off the island's east end and for young ladies in the casino ballroom.

Nowadays, **Catalina Express's** (☎ 310-519-1212) large and fast boats run several times daily from Ports of Call (San Pedro), Long Beach Harbor and Dana Point Marina to Avalon (the main town on the east end of the island). The Express also runs from Ports of Call to Isthmus Harbor. The trip is inexpensive and convenient, but you might want to buy your tickets early or make a reservation on summer weekends and holidays, when Avalon crawls with tourists.

Avalon's summer crowds are diverse, but usually mellow. During much of the winter many restaurants and shops shut down and the town is often delightfully empty. The fleets of diving, fishing and sightseeing boats operate year-round.

Two Harbors, the town on the tiny strip of land between Isthmus Harbor (front side) and Cat Harbor (back side), is much smaller than Avalon and is less crowded and less touristy. Most people get there on their own boats. There's only one real restaurant, a small marina and dive shop, a youth hostel, one rustic hotel and some nearby campsites.

In 1975 the **Santa Catalina Island Conservancy** (☎ 310-510-1421, www .catalinaconservancy.org) acquired title to 88% of the island's real estate. The conservancy is a private, nonprofit organization whose mission is to preserve, restore and protect the island and its surrounding waters.

An old network of ranch service roads extends all over the island. On some of these, hiking and bicycling is allowed. Hikers must obtain a permit (free), map and a list of regulations. These are available at the Conservancy House in Avalon, the Wrigley Memorial & Botanical Gardens, the Hermit Gulch Campgrounds or the Airport in the Sky (a tiny airstrip near the Isthmus). The conservancy offers guided hiking and camping tours of the interior. Hikers can expect to see island foxes, as well as all sorts of birds and marine mammals. In the hills above the Isthmus there's a small herd of bison.

To camp on Catalina, contact the Santa Catalina Island Conservancy or the **Catalina Island Company** (☎ 310-510-0344), which owns the remainder of the island and manages two major campgrounds, Hermit Gulch and Two Harbors. A shuttle that runs between Avalon and the airport services some of the main campsites on the island.

Cyclists wishing to enter the interior must obtain a permit for a nominal fee. You can rent mopeds and motor scooters (but not cars) in Avalon, but you can't operate them in the interior of the island.

Several Avalon hotels cater specifically to divers. They provide drying racks in their courtyards and gear cartage to and from the boat landings and Avalon Underwater Park. These are not necessarily four-star establishments—as a rule they don't serve food, but there are plenty of places to eat within a short walk.

Most of these hotels offer package deals that combine passage on the Express, two or three nights' accommodations, on-board meals and boat diving and/or beach diving (sometimes with guides). A package deal serves well as both an introduction to Southern California diving and a pleasant, inexpensive vacation.

The landmark Catalina Casino houses a movie theater and ballroom. It was named for the Italian word for "place of gathering or entertainment"—it never was a gambling venue.

Diving Health & Safety

BONNIE CARDONE

General Health

California is a relatively safe place to travel, generally free of unusual endemic diseases or other special health risks. Emergency and medical facilities are readily accessible.

Most health risks associated with diving are easy to prevent or avoid. Keep yourself warm, both in and out of the water. Exercise care on entries and exits, especially at shore sites. To avoid sunburn and dehydration, use sunscreen and drink lots of water.

Dive conservatively. Don't push your depth and bottom time limits, and make controlled ascents and safety stops. Make the outbound leg of your dive against the current. Use underwater navigation skills to avoid the need for long surface swims. Don't use up all your air during a dive, especially in kelpy areas—keep at least 500 psi in your tank to enable you to return underwater to the swim step at the stern of the boat, thus avoiding kelp entanglement.

Enriched Air Diving

Enriched air, or nitrox, has become increasingly popular with experienced Southern California divers in recent years. In the 50 to 100ft (15 to 30m) range, enriched air can significantly extend no-decompression limits.

There are risks, however. The increased percentage of oxygen can cause a toxic reaction, especially at extreme depth. Before you can obtain enriched air from a shop or boat, you must pass an accredited EA/Nitrox course and get a nitrox C-card. Also, your dedicated nitrox tank must display EA/Nitrox decals from PADI or another accredited agency.

Originally, enriched air mixes were produced by pumping pure oxygen into tanks or air banks containing normal air (21% oxygen) until the desired concentration was achieved. Pure oxygen is highly volatile and tends to combine with all sorts of substances, including metals and neoprene. As a result, scuba tanks and regulators (even BCs) had to be specially redesigned for enriched air. Outfitting oneself for nitrox used to be rather expensive.

Recent advances have made it possible to use enriched air without purchasing special equipment. Now, many enriched air systems filter nitrogen from normal air, rather than pumping in oxygen. Enriched air filtration systems enable divers to use nitrox with no special equipment, other than a dedicated tank. An enriched air diving computer, while not a necessity, is a great convenience.

Pre-Trip Preparation

Honestly assess your general health, diving skills and equipment. If you're out of shape, start exercising. If you haven't dived in more than six months or if you have never dived in cold water, take a scuba review course and get accustomed to wearing a 7mm wetsuit with a hood and using the corresponding weight.

If you don't already have one, install a compass with a lubber line on your instrument console and practice until you are confident navigating with less than 30ft (9m) of visibility. If you don't feel confident about your navigational skills, you may be too worried about returning to the boat to enjoy your dive.

KATHY DEWET-OLESON

Check your equipment thoroughly before setting out for a dive.

Many Southern California dive instructors and divemasters will take you on a checkout dive to prepare you for local conditions. To arrange this, simply contact your certifying agency or any accredited dive shop.

If you're using your own dive gear (regulator, BC, computer and so forth), have it serviced at least once a year, even if you don't dive very often. If you dive less than once a year, service your gear shortly before the trip.

Make your own save-a-dive kit. Include fin straps, mask straps, o-rings, snorkel retainers, regulator mouthpiece, neoprene cement, silicone gel, zip ties, duct tape, cyalume light sticks, dive-light batteries, a spare computer

Buoyancy Skills

Lack of buoyancy control can make diving far less pleasurable, even unsafe. If you haven't worn a 7mm wetsuit or a drysuit before, make some practice dives in a controlled environment. Find out how much weight you need to wear in order to descend and ascend under control. A perfectly weighted diver should have no difficulty maintaining neutral buoyancy at 15ft (4.5m) at the end of the dive.

Due to anxiety and the air trapped inside your wetsuit before a dive, you may have difficulty descending at first. To compensate, you may want to add too much weight. Resist that temptation—it's risky and unnecessary. If you kick down vigorously on your first descent, the added pressure will compress the trapped gas in your wetsuit within a few feet of the surface, making you less buoyant. Wearing too much weight can cause you to descend out of control. On ascent, too much weight can cause you to strain, tire, even hyperventilate in extreme cases.

For proper weighting with a 7mm wetsuit, use 10% of your body weight as a baseline figure. Add or subtract weight in 1 to 2lb (.5 to 1kg) increments until you find the right amount. Make sure your BC has enough lifting capacity to handle the weight.

battery, maybe a spare mask, a couple of screwdrivers and wrenches. Also have a basic first-aid kit (including motion sickness tablets if needed). For in-water emergencies, be sure to have a whistle and an inflatable safety tube clipped to your BC.

DAN

Divers Alert Network (DAN) is an international membership association of individuals and organizations sharing a common interest in diving and safety. It operates a 24-hour diving emergency hotline in the U.S.: ☎ 919-684-8111 or 919-684-4DAN (-4326). The latter accepts collect calls in a dive emergency. Though DAN does not directly provide medical care, it does provide advice on early treatment, evacuation and hyperbaric treatment of diving-related injuries.

DAN membership is reasonably priced and includes DAN TravelAssist, a membership benefit that covers medical air evacuation from anywhere in the world for any illness or injury. For a small additional fee, divers can get secondary insurance coverage for decompression illness. For membership details contact DAN at ☎ 800-446-2671 in the U.S. or ☎ 919-684-2948 elsewhere. DAN can also be reached at www.diversalertnetwork.org.

Diving Emergency Plan

Each diver should have a simple emergency preparedness plan, utilizing readily available local resources. In a medical emergency call ☎ 911 to activate the Emergency Medical Services. Even if you suspect that recompression may be needed, do not go directly to a recompression chamber. There are a number of reasons why going to the nearest chamber first is not the best course of action. Most chambers require a referral from a physician or DAN before accepting a dive patient. Also, the availability of a chamber can change from week to week or day to day. Although chambers keep DAN informed of their operational status, this information is not generally made public.

In case of a diving emergency, DAN recommends:
1. Establish (A)irway, (B)reathing, (C)irculation.
2. In the case of hyperbaric injury, give 100% oxygen.
3. Contact local EMS at ☎ 911 for transport to the nearest hospital.
4. Contact DAN at ☎ 919-684-8111 or 919-684-4DAN (collect). A medical diagnosis of a diving injury should not be made in the field but should be treated with standard first aid until the case is turned over to medical professionals.

If you have a diving-related injury or other medical problem as a passenger on a diving charter boat, report your condition to a crew member. From that point, the matter will be largely out of your hands. If your symptoms warrant it, the charter operator will follow the above procedures. If necessary, the U.S. Coast Guard (or a civilian medivac unit) will transport you to the nearest appropriate facility.

Diving in Southern Califoria

DAVID MCCRAY

Southern California's marine environment offers divers the opportunity to observe an amazing variety of wild-life and topography. Miles offshore, seamounts rise from astonishing depths, every square inch of surface area covered with scallops, anemones, sea stars, sponges, feather duster worms and tunicates. In golden kelp groves, sea lions and harbor seals swoop and glide, trailing streams of bubbles.

Bizarre and colorful tiny fish and nudibranchs hide in the cracks of rocky reefs. Bright red rockfish hover over deep structures. Nearby, toothy green lingcod guard their nesting ledges. In the distance, a squadron of bat rays glides effortlessly over the sand.

Roving schools of yellowtail and barracuda attack glittering balls of baitfish in mid-water. White sea bass doze beneath the kelp canopy. Huge, majestic black sea bass magically appear in the open water outside a kelpy reef, placidly look you over and swim on.

Map Index

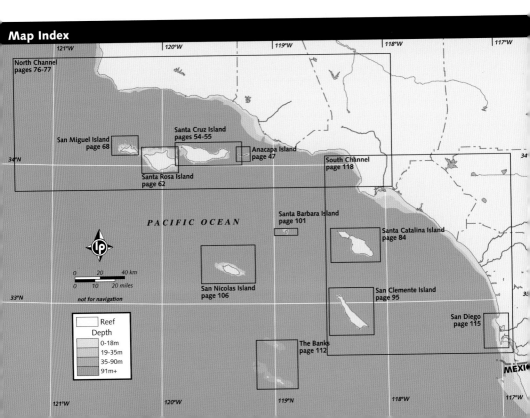

PACIFIC OCEAN

0   20   40 km
0   10   20 miles
not for navigation

Reef
Depth
0-18m
19-35m
35-90m
91m+

MEXI

On moonlit nights squid ascend from ancient marine trenches to spawn and lay their tubular eggs in sandy coves. On calm afternoons blue sharks fin lazily at the surface in mid-channel. Blue and humpback whales come to the Santa Barbara Channel to feed on krill in summer. Gray whales move through in winter on their way to calve and mate off Baja California, Mexico. Huge pods of porpoises remain in Southern California waters year-round, hunting baitfish and mackerel.

The North Channel Islands—Anacapa, Santa Cruz, Santa Rosa and San Miguel—form a geographically distinct group, separated from the mainland by the . Santa Barbara Channel. The Southern Channel Islands are Santa Catalina, Santa Barbara, San Nicolas and San Clemente. Also within that group are Cortes Bank (a vast seamount 100 miles offshore) and the inshore area around San Diego. The San Pedro Channel lies between the South Islands and L.A. County, while the Gulf of Santa Catalina separates them from the San Diego County coastline.

Dive boats based in Santa Barbara and Ventura frequent the North Islands, while San Pedro, Long Beach and San Diego boats commonly visit the South Islands.

Diving in the North Channel Islands

Anacapa, Santa Cruz, Santa Rosa and San Miguel run east to west in a 70-mile chain. On a clear day, all four are visible from the bluffs a few miles west of the city of Santa Barbara. Together with tiny Santa Barbara Island (40 miles to the south), the North Islands make up the Channel Islands National Park, one of the most beautiful wild places left in North America.

Due to the influence of the California Current, the water surrounding the North Channel Islands tends to be colder than that of the South Channel. The weather is generally rougher, especially in winter and spring, when storms from Alaska and the Central Pacific pound the region. The North Channel Islands actually shelter some of the South Channel Islands and beaches from northern swells and storms.

BONNIE CARDONE

Protected anchorages, such as Scorpion's Anchorage above,
make for popular Channel Islands dive sites.

In calm periods during the fall and winter, water clarity is often better than it is during the summer due to lighter plankton bloom and the absence of a thermocline.

As you would expect, fish and invertebrate populations of the North Islands are somewhat distinct from those found in the south. Vermilion rockfish, copper rockfish, lingcod and red abalone—species that thrive in colder water—are more common in the North Channel, especially in the relatively shallow depths visited by recreational divers.

Most divers reach the North Islands on licensed dive charter boats based in Santa Barbara and Ventura. Dive charters run year-round, weather permitting. More trips get scrubbed due to bad weather in spring than in any other season.

Only experienced, properly equipped boaters should attempt to navigate in the North Channel Islands. Although the islands are usually visible from the mainland, high winds and swells can very quickly make the Santa Barbara Channel unsafe for small craft. While few private boaters dive in the outer islands (Santa Rosa and San Miguel), it is not beyond the abilities of an experienced small-boat owner to reach the front side of Santa Cruz from Santa Barbara or Ventura Harbor, or reach Anacapa Island from Ventura Harbor or Channel Islands Harbor in Oxnard. Visited less frequently, the outer islands remain wilder and more pristine than the inner islands.

Diving in the South Channel Islands

The waters of the South Channel, warmed by the California Countercurrent, can be downright balmy by local standards (more than 75°F, or 24°C, in summer). The warm waters and abundant food attract migratory pelagic fish like tuna and dorado from subtropical regions farther south.

Although exposed to storms from Mexico and the Equatorial Pacific, the South Channel is usually calmer than the north. Even when a strong southwest swell is pumping, the lee sides of Catalina and San Clemente provide many sheltered areas for safe diving. The back sides of Catalina and San Clemente, and every side of Santa Barbara and San Nicolas, are much more exposed to weather. Consequently, wind and swell conditions are usually rougher there.

At many remote sites such as Farnsworth Bank (Catalina), Nine Fathom Reef (San Clemente) and Cortes Bank, powerful currents ensure excellent water clarity by sweeping away the plankton. Moreover, due to their relative inaccessibility, the outer islands are wilder and less exploited—marine life of all types is more abundant. The outer islands of the southern region are often worth the long, sometimes uncomfortable boat trip from San Pedro, Long Beach or San Diego.

Diving from small private craft is more common in the South Channel Islands than up north. This is partly because the weather is usually calmer and more predictable, and partly because Catalina is close to many private marinas and public boat ramps in Los Angeles and Orange Counties. In fact, inexperienced or careless private boat operators pose a serious hazard to divers at mainland beach sites and around Catalina.

Boat Diving

Southern California's fleet of dive charter boats works year-round. The boats are busiest on weekends, but you can book a trip for any day of the week out of at least one of the main harbors: Santa Barbara, Ventura, Long Beach, San Pedro, Avalon or Mission Bay. There are a few dive charter boats based in Two Harbors (Catalina) and Huntington Harbor. As a rule, California dive boats are clean and comfortable, with helpful, professional crews.

Most of the larger boats have live-aboard capability and often book trips for two, three or even four days. Most of the multi-day trips are club charters. Space on club charter trips is generally closed to non-club members, but the club may open the trip if space becomes available.

Any trip to the outer islands will involve at least one night of on-board travel. Inner-island trips (or wreck dives in San Diego), called ½ day or ¾ day trips, often leave the dock in the early morning, but many boats allow you to sleep on-board at the dock if that is more convenient.

To plan their trips, many local divers rely on the California Scuba Calendar section of *California Diving News*, a free monthly newsprint publication available in most dive shops and online at www.saintbrendan.com.

Southern California boat diving is not like tropical-resort boat diving. Some of this relates to conditions, some of it to economics. Though you may be comfortable diving to 130ft (40m) in Cozumel or Grand Cayman, if you haven't mastered buoyancy control wearing a 7mm wetsuit and weights, you may ascend or descend too fast, overexert on ascent or even hyperventilate.

With few exceptions, Southern California dive boats do not provide underwater tour guides. There is nothing, however, to prevent you from hiring a local divemaster or instructor to accompany you on your first few cold-water dives.

Divemasters work the deck, fill tanks, check divers in and out, give technical advice and dive-site briefings, repair equipment (at their discretion) and stand by to make rescues or administer first aid. Boat operators expect you to dive safely and return to the boat unaided (unless you have an in-water

Dive boats can access unique sites, such as the Painted Cave on Santa Cruz.

KATHY DEWET-OLESON

Diving with Pinnipeds

Southern California divers frequently encounter pinnipeds, almost always California sea lions or harbor seals. Rarely threatening, these wild, marine predators often demonstrate curiosity about divers and even a willingness to interact with us.

Sea Lions Sea lions are otarids, or eared seals, related to fur seals. All otarids have a visible external ear flap. Their hind flippers are used to help them move fairly quickly on land. In the water their powerful front flippers propel them, like a penguin's wings. In the open ocean, otarids can swim at the surface with speed and grace.

In the spring breeding season more than 100,000 California sea lions (*Zalophus californianus*) throng the rookeries on San Miguel, San Nicolas and Santa Barbara Islands. Dark or golden brown in color, mature males weigh 700lbs (315kg), females about 240lbs (110kg). They feed primarily on fish.

Sea lions are social mammals but not particularly peaceful. Where they gather in large numbers, you can hear their barks and roars from miles away. In July the males head north to fatten up on salmon, but many females and juveniles remain in Southern California year-round. You may encounter them almost anywhere, any time of year.

Easily distinguished from females by their size and a cranial crest, only dominant males can attract a harem and then mate, which may account for their invariable pugnacity. If you unwittingly

DAVID MCCRAY

intrude into his territory, a male may suddenly dive at you from above. His canines are capable of inflicting serious wounds, but he is extremely unlikely to attack if you back off. However, male sea lions can be quite persistent about relieving a spearfisherman of his catch.

Delightfully friendly by comparison, juveniles seem to find divers absolutely fascinating. Near rookeries, gangs of them hit the water as soon as a dive boat drops anchor. They'll nip at your fins, mimic your movements and stare into your face plate. Females are also often curious about divers, if not utterly ecstatic like the juveniles. Not surprisingly, nursing females have bitten divers near birthing areas or nursery pools.

Northern Fur Seals Every winter, about 10,000 northern fur seals (*Callorhinus ursinus*) come to San Miguel to breed. They are smaller than California sea lions, with shorter snouts and denser fur. Males weigh about 500lbs (225kg), females about 150lbs (65kg). You'd be lucky to see one in the water—while at San Miguel they spend most of their time on land, fighting, breeding, birthing and nursing. Watch for the telltale stream of bubbles—their fur is thicker than sea lion fur and the air trapped in it escapes as tiny bubbles as they swim through the water.

Harbor Seals Like all phocids, harbor seals (*Phoca vitulina*) have no external ear flaps. Limited to wriggling on their stomachs on land, they take to the water at the first sign of danger. To swim, they use their rear flippers with a side-to-side pumping motion. They can't swim as fast as sea lions, but they are incredibly agile. Solitary hunters, acrobatic and nosy, harbor seals are usually mottled brown or black, or silver-grey with black spots.

There about 20,000 harbor seals in Southern California, living alone or in groups, rarely as many as a hundred individuals together, never in huge colonies like sea lions. They feed on fish, squid and crustaceans. Mature males weigh about 175lbs (80kg), females about 125lbs (55kg).

DAVID MCCRAY

By pinniped standards, harbor seals are shy and quiet. They almost never vocalize; occasionally, they may slap the water as a territorial display.

Harbor seals are curious about divers, sometimes following them at a discreet distance throughout a dive. Probably because many of their favorite prey items shelter in small caves or under ledges, their curiosity seems especially aroused when they see a diver poking around in a hole. If you don't know it's there, it can be a little disconcerting to turn around and confront a harbor seal's wide-eyed, whiskery face.

Northern Elephant Seals Also a phocid, the northern elephant seal (*Mirounga angustirostris*) is a true giant. Full-grown males weigh up to 2½ tons (2,250kg), females 900lbs (400kg). Besides their size, males are distinguished by a large proboscoid nasal chamber. On San Miguel and San Nicolas Islands during the fall and winter, the males haul out and joust for breeding territories, then the females arrive to give birth, nurse and mate.

Once slaughtered to the point of extinction, elephant seals are now protected. They number well over 10,000, all descendants of a few survivors left on Guadalupe Island off Baja California. In the 1960s they colonized Año Nuevo Island in Central California. Now they're all over the outer Channel Islands.

A favorite prey of orcas and great white sharks, they are vulnerable in shallow water. Elephant seals dive deep, up to half a mile, and stay deep for hours, sometimes even sleeping underwater. Scientists are still not sure how they do it. On the beach, young ones practice their breath-holding skills, lying as if dead for several minutes at a time. Divers rarely encounter elephant seals in the water, and there isn't much interaction when they do. Once you get over the shock of its size, it is a brief but memorable thrill.

ANDREW SALLMON

emergency), no matter the conditions. You are expected to monitor you own depth and bottom times.

The captain or a divemaster will give you a detailed pre-dive briefing but you must decide for yourself whether your skills are adequate for the site and the conditions. Before booking a trip, ask about the appropriate level of skill required to make most of the planned dives. You'll avoid sitting around on deck all day or pushing yourself beyond your abilities.

The key to an enjoyable dive-boat trip is simple: get on the right boat, with the right group, going to sites that suit your skills and interests. Members of dive clubs generally get a pretty good idea about each trip in their meetings, but if you're new to the area, or visiting, you will probably be booking space on open boats, not club charters. Open boats often accommodate specific types of customers: photographers and sightseers, free-divers, hunters, instructors and classes. On many dive boats booked primarily by scuba divers, free-divers get a reduced price since they don't need airfills.

Spearfishing, either free-diving or on scuba, and the taking of invertebrate game (mostly lobsters and scallops, now that the abalone fishery is closed), is still widely practiced and generally accepted by the Southern California diving community. If you would be uncomfortable around divers harvesting game, avoid boats that cater to hunters.

Ask if there are certification classes doing checkout dives on the trip. For safety, economy and convenience, many instructors book their classes on short-hop trips to sites known for clear, calm water and some nice scenery. If this would bore you, or you don't like the idea of stumbling over a herd of students on deck or in the water, avoid trips like this. On the other hand, if you're new to the area or a new diver, "student boats" may be an ideal introduction to Southern California boat diving.

Shore Diving

Beach diving in Southern California, while economical and sometimes a bit more convenient, is not usually as good as diving at the Channel Islands. Inshore sites are often exposed to wave action,

BONNIE CARDONE
A plastic tarp helps to keep dive gear clean when gearing up for a shore dive.

which makes entrances and exits more difficult and degrades water clarity by churning up the bottom sediment. Weather that would not significantly affect a boat-dive trip can make a colossal mess of a beach dive. Shore sites also suffer from pollution, competing recreational activities (private boats are a major hazard) and overfishing.

On a sandy beach, swells larger than 3ft (1m) can pose a hazard for divers in full scuba gear. On a rocky beach, smaller waves may make exits quite dangerous, even for snorkelers. Beach diving, which often requires long hikes carrying heavy gear, can be physically taxing under the best conditions. If you are a new diver, or new to Southern California diving, don't try shore diving without enlisting the assistance of a local, experienced beach diver, preferably a divemaster or an instructor. Local, accredited dive shops can arrange this.

On a good day, however, you can have a great dive if you choose the right site. By paying close attention to marine weather reports and consulting online resources like the Southern California Swell Model, you can get a fairly accurate picture of shore-diving conditions along the coast. Combine this information with a basic knowledge of local topography and you can reasonably assess your chances of finding a safe and enjoyable shore dive on any given day.

Swell Models

The Southern California Swell Model page (http://cdip.ucsd.edu/models/wave .model.shtml), a service of the University of California San Diego, is very helpful in deciding which beach sites are likely to be calm enough to dive. The summary information in the upper right-hand corner of the swell model tells you the average height of the waves, the frequency of the swells and the compass direction from which the waves are arriving. The colors on the map depict regional wave height. This information, combined with a basic understanding of the geographic location of a site, will help you determine its diveability.

The swell model image and data were furnished by the Coastal Data Information Program, operated by the Scripps Institution of Oceanography.

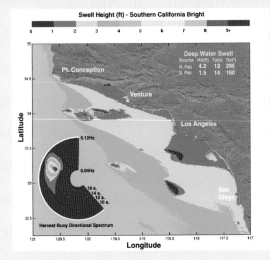

Snorkeling & Free-Diving

With the exception of the shallow ends of sheltered coves, there aren't too many places in Southern California where you can just snorkel along at the surface and see what's going on at or near the bottom. The water clarity, especially in the top few feet, is just not good enough most of the time. As you examine the dive site summary boxes, bear in mind that many, if not most, of the places where you see the snorkel icon are really free-diving sites.

A diver who practices breath-hold diving, or free-diving, can enter a world that scuba divers never see. The reason is simple: bubbles scare most fish away, probably because most of the things in the water that blow bubbles (pinnipeds and toothed whales, for example) also eat fish. Breath-hold diving is a silent discipline, allowing a diver to approach fish that would have already fled from a scuba diver.

At most beach sites (with the exception of the deep inshore canyons like La Jolla and Redondo, which are only accessible to scuba divers), free-diving may be preferable because you don't have to haul so much heavy gear. Another advantage: There is no time limit—you dive until you get tired or cold, not until your air runs out.

You don't need to be a world-class breath-hold diver to enjoy this sport, but it's a good idea to practice regularly, until you're comfortable staying down for at least 30 seconds at 30ft (9m). As you relax during the course of a day, you will find that your stamina will improve. With a little training, a decent swimmer in good cardiovascular condition should have no problem staying for a minute at 30ft (9m) or deeper.

There are hazards, however. If you push yourself too hard, you risk blacking out. More dangerous than shallow-water blackout are careless boaters and all Jet Ski riders. At inshore sites near harbors and boat ramps, snorkelers must keep a wary eye out for them.

DAVID MCCRAY

Free-divers may see species that are scared off by divers' bubbles.

Certification & Specialty Classes

With dozens of dive shops and hundreds of qualified instructors, Southern California is about as good a place to learn to dive as you can find. At most shops, Open Water certification ranges from $350 to $400 per person (including classes, pool sessions, boat and gear rentals, and certification fees, but excluding the purchase of snorkel, mask, booties, gloves and fins). In some places, group rates may run about $100 less; semi-private and private classes are often available for a higher fee.

Shark-Cage Diving

A few Southern California dive-charter operators provide divers with the opportunity to observe and photograph sharks at close range. The best way to find someone to take you shark-cage diving, aside from consulting *California Diving News*, is to ask at your local dive shop. If there's a properly equipped shark-diving boat in a nearby harbor, they'll know about it.

Since only one or two divers can occupy the cage at one time, shark-diving boats run limited passenger loads. With higher insurance costs and fewer passengers, shark-cage diving is more expensive than other types of diving: about $200 to $300 per day, depending on the size of the boat.

Usually, these trips leave the dock around 8am, travel to a site where they've consistently been able to attract sharks, and return in the early evening. Ideally, every diver will get at least two 30- to 45-minute periods in the cage with sharks in the area.

A divemaster escorts the diver to the cage, a few feet below the surface. On some boats a diver wearing chain mail hand-feeds the sharks. A few operators allow divers to exit the cage while the divemaster feeds the sharks from a sealed plastic bag, one chunk at a time.

Most shark-cage diving is done in deep water, well offshore, so the water clarity is usually excellent. No one can guarantee that sharks will show up, but with luck they start arriving within an hour after the bait goes in the water. It is not uncommon for a dozen graceful, elongated blue sharks (*Prionace glauca*), ranging from 4 to 10ft (1.2 to 3m) long, to cruise through during the day. Occasionally, a husky, snaggle-toothed, 6ft (1.8m) shortfin mako (*Isurus oxyrinchus*) may dash in, unnerving the smaller blues. More often than not, you will get a chance to take some dramatic photos, sometimes at very close range.

ANDREW SALLMON

Warm-water referrals allow students to complete classroom and pool sessions in California, then travel to a warm-water destination for certification dives (and a vacation) at an accredited dive resort.

Most shops and instructors also offer specialty courses like Underwater Photography, Deep Diving, Drift Diving, Buoyancy Control, Search & Recovery, Underwater Naturalist, Underwater Navigation, EA/Nitrox and Wreck Diving. Many shops offer a Drysuit Diving course free with a drysuit purchase.

For divers interested in entering the field of scuba instruction, each accrediting agency (NAUI, PADI, SSI, etc.) offers its own series of courses leading to Divemaster, Instructor and Master Instructor certification.

Dive Site Icons

The symbols at the beginning of each dive site description provide a quick summary of some of the important characteristics of each site:

 Good snorkeling or free-diving site.

 Remains or partial remains of a wreck can be seen at this site.

 Sheer wall or drop-off.

 Deep dive. Features of this dive are found in water deeper than 90ft (27m).

 Strong currents may be encountered at this site.

 Strong surge (the horizontal movement of water caused by waves) may be encountered at this site.

 Drift dive. Because of strong currents and/or difficulty in anchoring, a drift dive is recommended at this site.

 Shore dive. This site can be accessed from shore.

 Caves or caverns are a prominent feature of this site. Only experienced cave divers should explore inner cave areas.

 Marine preserve. Special protective regulations apply in this area.

Pisces Rating System for Dives & Divers

The dive sites in this book are rated according to the following diver skill-level rating system. These are not absolute ratings but apply to divers at a particular time, diving at a particular place. For instance, someone unfamiliar with prevailing conditions might be considered a novice diver at one dive area, but an intermediate diver at another, more familiar location.

Novice: A novice diver should be accompanied by an instructor, divemaster or advanced diver on all dives. A novice diver generally fits the following profile:
◆ basic scuba certification from an internationally recognized certifying agency
◆ dives infrequently (less than one trip a year)
◆ logged fewer than 25 total dives
◆ little or no experience diving in similar waters and conditions
◆ dives no deeper than 60ft (18m)

Intermediate: An intermediate diver generally fits the following profile:
◆ may have participated in some form of continuing diver education
◆ logged between 25 and 100 dives
◆ dives no deeper than 130ft (40m)
◆ has been diving in similar waters and conditions within the last six months

Advanced: An advanced diver generally fits the following profile:
◆ advanced certification
◆ has been diving for more than two years and logged over 100 dives
◆ has been diving in similar waters and conditions within the last six months

Regardless of your skill level, you should be in good physical condition and know your limitations. If you are uncertain of your own level of expertise for a particular site, ask the advice of a local dive instructor. He or she is best qualified to assess your abilities based on the site's prevailing dive conditions. Ultimately, however, you must decide if you are capable of making a particular dive, a decision that should take into account your level of training, recent experience and physical condition, as well as the conditions at the site. Remember that conditions can change at any time, even during a dive.

Anacapa Island Dive Sites

Barely half a mile (.8km) at its widest point and 5 miles (8km) from end to end, Anacapa is really three tiny islands. A hundred yards (90m) separates East from Middle Anacapa. You have to look hard to find the break between the Middle and West islands.

A two-hour boat ride south from Ventura Harbor, Anacapa is actually southeast of Santa Barbara. More than 60 miles (95km) east of Point Conception, Anacapa is completely sheltered from the north swell. Santa Cruz Island protects her from the west. The back side, exposed to southern storms, sometimes falls within the lee of San Nicolas Island.

Although Anacapa is not immune to plankton blooms and roaring currents, on most days it offers the prettiest diving conditions in the North Channel. Visibility often extends to 50ft (15m) and may approach 100ft (30m). Usually, the water is at least 5°F (3°C) warmer than at the outer islands.

In the quiet coves, kelpy grottoes and clear water of the East Anacapa Island Natural Area & Ecological Reserve, many fish allow divers to observe them at close range. The entire north side of East Anacapa from Arch Rock to the west end of East Anacapa Island (including Arch Rock and Cathedral Cove dive sites) is a no-take zone out to depths of 60ft (18m). In the reserve you'll find the boldest lobsters in California and the largest populations of red abalone east of San Miguel.

Anacapa Island Ecological Reserve is on the north side of Middle Anacapa Island from Keyhole Rock to the east end of Middle Anacapa Island, and the south side of West Anacapa from the isthmus to within a few yards of Cat Rock. No invertebrates may be taken from 20ft (6m) or less.

Anacapa Island Dive Sites	Good Snorkeling	Novice	Intermediate	Advanced
1 Arch Rock				●
2 Cathedral Cove	●	●		
3 The Goldfish Bowl	●	●		
4 Coral Reef			●	
5 Cat Rock	●	●		
6 Oil Platform Grace				●

Arch Rock and Coral Reef are among Anacapa's best-known deep dives. Look up occasionally, or you may miss the huge schools of yellowtail that seem to circle the island endlessly. Dense schools of blue rockfish are common in the exceptional clarity of the middle depths at The Goldfish Bowl, Cat Rock and The Underwater Island. Calico bass, garibaldi, opaleye and surfperch lurk in the shallow rocks, underwater archways and kelp caverns at Cathedral Cove and nearby Landing Cove.

For snorkeling or free-diving, or for novices and divers unfamiliar with North Channel conditions, Anacapa Island is the ideal destination.

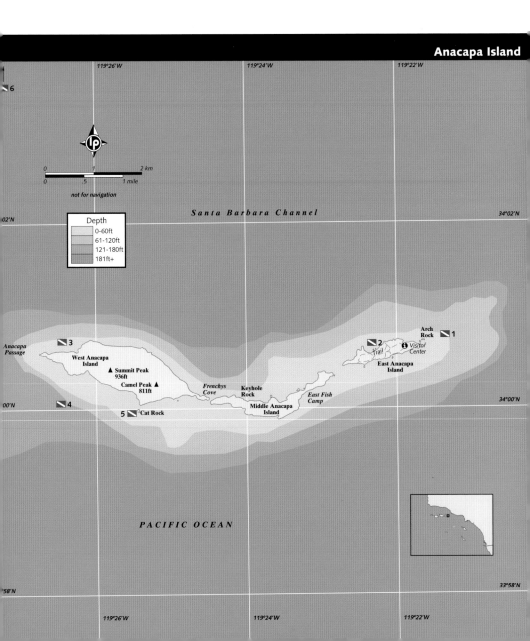

Anacapa Island

1 Arch Rock

The dramatic, often-photographed formation Arch Rock is perhaps the best-known bit of landscape in Channel Islands National Park. Underwater the Arch Rock dive site consists of a group of reefs and pinnacles that rise steeply from a rocky bottom at around 80ft.

Current, wind and swell conditions determine where a boat may safely anchor and, therefore, which part of these structures its divers will visit. In winter and spring the strong current around Arch Rock often precludes diving. In the calm of late summer and fall your chances

Location: About 100 yards (91m) E of East Anacapa Island

Depth Range: 50-80ft (15-24m)

Access: Boat

Expertise Rating: Advanced

are best. Considering the current, it's not a particularly good place to snorkel.

Arch Rock is not the clearest site on the island, but you'll usually find the site's best visibility (between 20 and 40ft) below the thermocline.

Arch Rock lies within the East Anacapa Reserve, which means that you may not remove or even touch anything. Consequently, invertebrate populations, which were once severely depleted, have been restored to a fairly healthy state. Large scallops and red abalone are common.

Photographers can find excellent macro subjects, such as anemones, nudibranchs and gorgonians. There's a sea lion rookery nearby, so you're almost certain to have pinniped company. Overall, it's a beautiful dive.

DAVID MCCRAY
Garibaldi are seen throughout Southern California.

2 Cathedral Cove

New divers, or those new to Southern California, will usually find comfortable conditions and excellent sightseeing at Cathedral Cove, on the front side of East Anacapa. You may encounter surge in the shallows, but conditions are generally quite mild. In fact, many Open Water students do their checkout dives in Cathedral Cove.

Location: Front side of East Anacapa Island

Depth Range: 10-50ft (3-15m)

Access: Boat

Expertise Rating: Novice

Garibaldi, surfperch, sheephead, senoritas and opaleye throng around the large rock near the entrance of the cove. Several healthy patches of kelp also grow from the rock piles in the 30ft depths. Harbor seals and sea lions haul out on the rocky beach.

Cathedral Cove is inside the East Anacapa Reserve, a year-round "no-take" zone. Within the reserve, red abalone have made a decent come-back and lobsters are utterly fearless. Large calico bass, unapproachably wary in most places, let you to swim right up to them in the kelp grottoes, shallow caves and underwater arch-ways amid the inshore rocks.

One such passage, about 20ft long, leads into the next cove to the west. A moderately competent breath-hold diver can easily make it from one end to the other. With decent water clarity, lots of fish and no boat traffic or cur-rents, Cathedral Cove is an excellent snorkeling site. **Landing Cove**, a quar-ter mile east, offers similar conditions and sightseeing opportunities.

KATHY DEWET-OLESON

The protected Cathedral Cove is a popular site for checkout dives.

3 The Goldfish Bowl

A shallow reef extends perhaps 100 yards beyond land's end on the front side of West Anacapa, where cliffs rise sharply from the waterline. In the sheltered area between the outer reef edge and the cliffs is The Goldfish Bowl, a dive site equally suitable for snorkeling or scuba diving.

Probably because the Santa Barbara Channel and Anacapa Passage currents collide nearby, the Bowl is invariably full of fish—large schools of blue rockfish in mid-water, garibaldi, sheephead and cal-ico bass amid the rocks, and bat rays on the sand.

Location: Front side of West Anacapa Island

Depth Range: 10-60ft (3-18m)

Access: Boat

Expertise Rating: Novice

To avoid the current, which can be pretty stiff as close as 50 yards from the beach, most divers head for the sun-lit shallows east of the point. When the current is ripping, this is an intermediate site. When it is not, it's suitable for novice divers.

Farther east, where the island wall descends steeply below the surface, you can snorkel 10 yards offshore in 50 or 60ft of clear blue water. It's a great place to practice your free-diving skills while hoping to catch a glimpse of a giant black sea bass.

Northward, away from shore, the terrain changes from reef to sandy bottom. This is a good place to look for halibut. Over the deeper parts of the reef, at about 60 to 70ft, keep your eyes peeled for roving schools of yellowtail.

A curious garibaldi peeks from behind the shelter of a red gorgonian at The Goldfish Bowl.

4 Coral Reef

Strikingly beautiful, Coral Reef is Anacapa's best-known deep dive. The shallow end of the reef is marked by dense kelp growth. On the inshore side, two rocky structures, each about 100 yards wide, are separated by a sand channel.

Beneath the kelp the terrain is a jumble of rocks sloping gradually seaward. At around 40 to 50ft both fingers terminate abruptly at a vertical wall that plunges to the sand at 90 to 100ft. Look for lobsters in small caves along the base of the wall.

Location: Back side of West Anacapa Island

Depth Range: 20-100ft (6-30m)

Access: Boat

Expertise Rating: Intermediate

For macrophotography, Coral Reef rivals San Nicolas Island's Begg Rock and the Front Side Seamounts of San Miguel, which are known for their profusion of

Giant Sea Bass

The giant sea bass (*Stereolepis gigas*), which can grow to 7ft (2m) and more than 500lbs (225kg), is the largest bony fish to inhabit California waters. Their habitat ranges from Humboldt Bay to the Sea of Cortez, but they are most common from Point Conception southward. They are also known as black sea bass and jewfish.

They occupy inshore waters to depths of at least 150ft (45m). Adults usually live over rocky terrain and in kelp beds; juveniles may also frequent sandy habitats. Coloration varies from silver with dark spots to an almost uniform dark black or a silvery bronze. Juveniles go through a red phase and have a rounded tail fin.

Giant sea bass were once relatively common in Southern California, but their size made them trophy fish. By the 1970s, spearfishing, sportfishing and commercial fishing had substantially reduced the California population. Since 1982 the species has been protected in California from recreational and commercial harvests.

Sightings of large adult sea bass remain rare, but appear to be increasing each year. In the mid '90s, the species showed signs of a modest comeback. Seasonal aggregations of adults and sub-adults were seen at Anacapa, Catalina and Santa Barbara Islands.

Divers encounter giant sea bass most often in the summer, when these fish aggregate in shallow water. Peak aggregations of up to 30 individuals occur in July and August, which is believed to be the spawning season. Though giant sea bass are somewhat territorial at this time, they are not guarding nesting areas. They are oviparous—they spawn, and the young develop outside the female in open water. A spawning pair circles each other intently, then rapidly swims upward in a spawning ascent. Currently, aggregation sites are being identified around the Channel Islands and a few inshore mainland locations.

Giant sea bass can be observed closely if approached with slow, non-threatening movements. Often, giant sea bass will initiate close contact by swimming toward a diver for a closer look. Most of them are infested to some degree with copepods around the face and gills. Divers have observed many types of interactions between giant sea bass and small

fish (often juveniles) that provide cleaner services. Though sightings of giant sea bass have become more common, divers rarely see them in winter. Where the fish go after the summer aggregations remains a mystery that scientists seek to answer.

For up-to-date information on giant sea bass observations and research, log on to www.cinms.nos.noaa.gov/gtseabass.stm and www.pier.org.

—*Kathy deWet-Oleson*

sessile marine life. Below 60ft, gorgonians, cup corals, sea strawberries, brittle stars and strawberry anemones carpet the rock. To see the true colors of the invertebrates, bring a dive light.

Conditions here vary, especially the current. If it's running hard, this is an advanced site. There may be a plankton bloom above the thermocline, but it generally clears below 60ft.

A rainbow-colored brittle star sits atop a giant star, *Piaster giganteus*.

5 Cat Rock

Protected from the north swell by the main body of the island, Cat Rock rises steeply from 60ft to break the surface about 50 yards offshore. Depending on which way the current is running, dive boats anchor either to the east or west of the rock, which is near the center of the quarter-mile-long reef. This site is appropriate for divers of all abilities, unless there is a strong current running.

Location: Back side of West Anacapa Island

Depth Range: 10-60ft (3-18m)

Access: Boat

Expertise Rating: Novice

Cat Rock is great for snorkeling. Crawl quietly through the shallow kelpy pools along the shore and you may surprise a snoozing white sea bass. A narrow, boulder-strewn channel separates Cat Rock from the island. Like the inshore pools, it tends to be surgey, but calico bass seem to like it.

A patchwork of kelp stands, small caves and grottoes, finger reefs, sand channels and short walls, the reef is an ideal fish habitat. In summer, halibut spawn in the sandy areas. A dozen species of perch, rockfish and wrasses flit and hover amid the rocks. Bat rays frequent the cove to the west of Cat Rock year-round. Schools of yellowtail patrol the deeper water. On a sunny day this place is golden.

Less than a half mile west, a lovely little reef called **The Underwater Island** is in 60ft of water and surrounded by sand. If you dive Cat Rock, chances are good that you will also dive this reef. Swarming with fish and carpeted with invertebrates, Underwater Island rises to within 30ft of the surface. It's no chore for scuba divers to swim all the way around it in a single dive.

6 | Oil Platform Grace

Since the 1960s nearly 20 offshore platforms have been pumping oil through a pipeline to a refinery near the city of Santa Barbara. After a large spill soiled area beaches in 1982—killing seabirds, marine mammals and fish—Congress prohibited any new drilling platforms from being built in the channel and mandated improved safety and cleanup systems. Since then there have been no major spills, but you often see globs of coagulated oil floating in the channel.

Dive boats are allowed to visit Grace, an inactive drilling platform that now serves as a pumping station.

Standing in more than 200ft of nutrient-rich water, the platform's massive legs and braces make ideal homes for the benthic adult stages of free-swimming larval zooplankton. Photographers can choose from an astonishing array of colorful sponges and mollusks. Among locals, the rigs are famous for an easy harvest of jumbo scallops.

The rigs provide shelter to sizeable resident populations of blue and olive rockfish and calico bass. Sea lions hunt the fish and haul out on the catwalks. Schools of baitfish and roving pelagics, such as yellowtail, mola-molas and blue sharks, drift in from time to time. On a good day, vertical visibility may exceed 100ft, which makes for great wide-angle shots of divers or large critters profiled against the invertebrate-encrusted structure.

The structures compress the swell on the down-current side, which can make the swim-step

Location: Between Ventura Harbor and the east end of Santa Cruz Island

Depth Range: 30-130ft (9.1-40m)

Access: Boat

Expertise Rating: Advanced

exit somewhat adventurous. Considering this and the depths involved, the oil platforms are advanced dive sites. Follow the pre-dive briefing instructions and closely monitor your depth and bottom time.

BONNIE CARDONE

Invertebrates encrust the oil platform's pilings.

Santa Cruz Island Dive Sites

At 25 miles (40km) long, Santa Cruz is the largest of the North Channel Islands. Almost any point on the front side is about a two-and-a-half-hour boat ride from Santa Barbara. From Ventura Harbor to the east end is perhaps two hours.

Although Point Conception shields Santa Cruz from the north swell, strong currents and severe wind chop adversely affect diving conditions west of Chinese Harbor all the way to Morse Point. Although the coves may offer safe anchorage, visibility is often less than 10ft (3m). This is a shame, because this stretch of coastline offers several spectacular wall dives, a series of delightful coves and the mystical Painted Cave. To dive them under good conditions, you have to get lucky.

The back side and east end are also open to the current, but the swell and air are usually calmer than on the front side. Gull Island is the westernmost sheltered site on the back side. If Gull is blown out, Willows Anchorage will probably be calm. On the east end, from Albert's Anchorage to Scorpion's Anchorage, you may catch the wraparound current roaring through the Anacapa Passage. Listen closely to the pre-dive briefings. If the captain tells you to hug the wall, he means it.

That said, diving at Santa Cruz is often wonderful. The water is usually a few degrees warmer than at Santa Rosa or San Miguel. The inshore reefs at Valley Anchorage, The Radar Towers and Yellowbanks are colorful and serene.

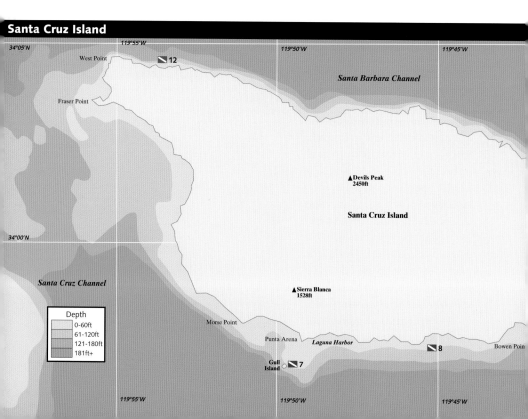

Santa Cruz Island

Squid spawn here nearly year-round, attracting roving schools of yellowtail, barracuda, mackerel and white sea bass (especially at Chinese Harbor) and keeping the local halibut, calico bass, sea lions and harbor seals fat and happy. You may find game fish and pinnipeds at practically any site or at any depth.

Santa Cruz boasts a growing population of black sea bass. You may encounter these placid giants socializing on a rocky reef at Willows or nibbling squid eggs at Scorpion's. In summer, bring your wide-angle lens and cross your fingers.

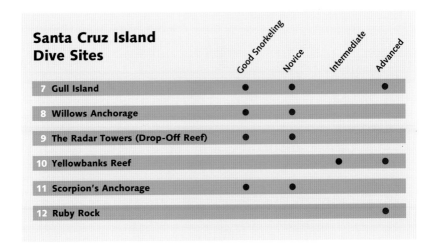

Santa Cruz Island Dive Sites	Good Snorkeling	Novice	Intermediate	Advanced
7 Gull Island	●	●		●
8 Willows Anchorage	●	●		
9 The Radar Towers (Drop-Off Reef)	●	●		
10 Yellowbanks Reef			●	●
11 Scorpion's Anchorage	●	●		
12 Ruby Rock				●

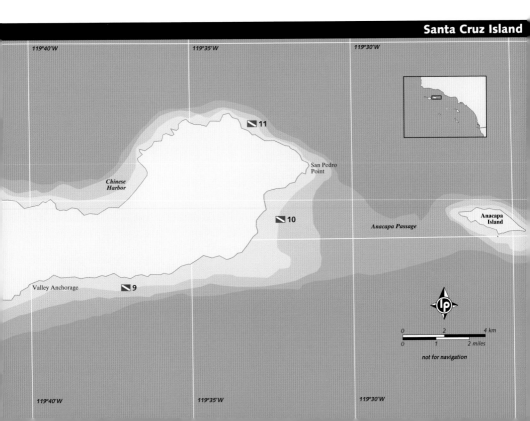

7 Gull Island

Gull Island is actually a complex seamount with several pinnacles, some of which break the surface. The largest pinnacle forms the main island, the reef that surrounds it, and a rocky islet a short distance to the northeast.

About a quarter mile southeast of the main island, another branch of the structure rises from 120 to 10ft. On the seaward side a series of ledges descends to about 50ft, where a steep wall careens to meet the sandy bottom.

In the sand around these rocks, you may find clusters of white tubular squid eggs. A mile southwest of Gull the bottom falls away to 1,200ft. When squid rise from these depths to spawn and lay eggs in shallow bays, they attract everything that likes to eat them: white sea bass, yellowtail, halibut, lingcod, calico bass and the larger rockfish species, as well as invertebrates such as crabs. With the exception of white sea bass, you may encounter all of these on or over the deeper parts of the reef.

Gull Island has a great reputation among spearfishermen as a place where white sea bass school in the spring and

Location: Back side of Santa Cruz, SW of Punta Arena

Depth Range: 20-120ft (6-37m)

Access: Boat

Expertise Rating: Novice (inside reef) Advanced (wall)

early summer. To get close to this elusive game fish, you must snorkel very quietly through the kelp canopy.

The series of rocky mounds around the island make a great shallow dive, although the surge can be severe. Large numbers of calico bass and olive rockfish inhabit this kelpy reef, along with the usual aggregation of opaleye, sheephead and surfperch. On the island side there's a short wall where you can sometimes find some very crowded lobster holes.

Depth and current make the wall an advanced site. On a dead-calm day, anyone can dive the inside reef, but when the surge is up, it's not suitable for novices.

DAVID MCCRAY

Slender crabs are one of many species that feast on squid eggs.

8   Willows Anchorage

When the northwest swell is pounding or the Santa Ana wind is whipping off the high desert, dive boats may take shelter in Willows Anchorage. Because it's sheltered and shallow, Willows is usually calm and clear—a lovely place to dive.

With its steep inshore walls, sandy bottom in the middle and extensive shallow reef near the entrance, Willows offers a variety of terrain and habitat equally suitable for snorkeling or scuba diving.

Although nearly devoid of kelp cover, the shallow reef is home to a large population of calico bass. Near the eastern end of the reef, boilers and a few rocks break the surface. East of the boilers the reef drops off to about 50ft.

One spearfishing free-diver claims to have hand-fed three young, 50lb black sea bass along this sloping wall several years ago. Sportfishermen have reported catching and, thankfully, releasing these "three brothers" at various points around Santa Cruz and Anacapa for years.

The usual complement of sheephead, opaleye perch, senorita wrasses and garibaldi live in and around the reef and inshore

Location: Back side of Santa Cruz, midway between Laguna Harbor & Bowen Pt.

Depth Range: 20-50ft (6-15m)

Access: Boat

Expertise Rating: Novice

walls of Willows Anchorage. If you look carefully at the sand you may find halibut, guitarfish, angel sharks, bat rays, sand bass, sheep crabs and nesting calico bass. In this area, however, keep an eye peeled for boat traffic.

KATHY DEWET-OLESON

Lucky divers may catch a glimpse of a giant black sea bass.

9   The Radar Towers (Drop-Off Reef)

East of Valley Anchorage, a group of radar towers sits atop a cliff that overlooks a mile-long reef system with three possible anchorages. Drop-Off Reef, the middle site, is perhaps the most interesting, but they all feature clear, calm, shallow water, golden kelp, fascinating topography and lots of fish. All are suitable for scuba diving and snorkeling.

Location: Back side of Santa Cruz, E of Valley Anchorage

Depth Range: 20-60ft (6-18m)

Access: Boat

Expertise Rating: Novice

At the eastern end of Drop-Off Reef, a kelp-covered, rocky mound extends for perhaps 50 yards perpendicular to the island, sheltering the site from the Anacapa Passage current. In mid-water, olive rockfish hide amid the kelp fronds, hoping to ambush baitfish.

Facing seaward, a wall rises from a sandy bottom at 60ft to between 20 and 30ft. In some places the wall is nearly vertical; in others it slopes from ledge to ledge. The structure is riddled with small caves, cracks, chimneys and channels. It's possible to crawl through some of these in scuba gear. In others it's possible to get stuck. They are worth carefully exploring, however, because large sheephead, calico bass and the occasional lobster hole up in these places during the day. One diver claims to have seen a 200lb black sea bass suck a lobster out of a hole on this reef.

Harbor seals hunt here all the time. If you peer into a small cavity in the reef, one of these curious pinnipeds may be unable to resist looking over your shoulder to find out what you're looking at. You'll often see bat rays on the sand in front of the reef, and a few sheep crabs almost always lumber into view.

10 Yellowbanks Reef

A wide area below tall, yellow cliffs, Yellowbanks Reef descends gradually, ledge by ledge, from inshore boilers to 120ft nearly 2 miles out—smack dab in the middle of the Anacapa Passage.

Most always, the deeper and farther out you get, the stiffer the current is. Below 90ft (about a mile out) it's usually more than 1.5 knots—too fast for safe scuba diving. Once in a great while, how-

Location: Back side of Santa Cruz, SW of San Pedro Pt.

Depth Range: 40-120ft (12-37m)

Access: Boat

Expertise Rating: Intermediate (shallow reef), Advanced (deeper reaches)

ever, a dive boat captain will allow a small group of advanced divers to drift along the outside reef. It's quite an experience.

Dozens of short and a few legal-sized lobsters cluster beneath the narrow ledges. As curious sheephead, ocean whitefish, rockfish and calico bass watch you tumble down-current, you can make out lobster antennae from 20 or 30ft away in the clear, deep water.

Yellowbanks' outside reef is one of the few remaining sites, outside of the East Anacapa Reserve and San Miguel Island, where you may still find red abalone clinging to the rocks.

ANDREW SALLMON
A gray moon sponge shelters a gopher rockfish.

On the shallower ledges you'll see many of the same critters (except for abalone) that are found in the depths, but fewer of them. For photographers, there are plenty of the usual reef invertebrate subjects, such as scallops, nudibranchs and anemones. The current keeps the water pretty clean here, although in summer there may be a plankton bloom near the surface. Even at 40 or 50ft the current can be difficult, but above 60ft Yellowbanks is usually an intermediate-level dive.

11 Scorpion's Anchorage

The east end of Santa Cruz is a roughly triangular headland, connected to the west end by a narrow neck. From Potato Harbor on the north side all the way around to Smuggler's Cove on the southeast side, a string of shallow coves offers shelter from the wind and swell.

Facing northeast, Scorpion's Anchorage is often the calmest of these. Two islets divide the main harbor from **Little Scorpion's**, directly to the southeast. The harbor walls are sloping rock piles, and there is a small kelp stand near the beach, but most of the bottom is muddy sand. Totally unlike the amber kelp forest of the invertebrate-encrusted deep reef, the sandy cove has its own unique charm.

All around Santa Cruz, squid rise at night from deep water to lay their eggs in the sand of these shallow bays. Just about everything in the ocean eats squid or squid eggs—cormorants, halibut, harbor seals, calico bass, rockfish, white sea bass, black sea bass, yellowtail, blue sharks and angel sharks. You may see any or all of these at Scorpion's.

Wherever you find squid eggs, look for aggregations of fish, such as calico bass, ocean

Location: East end of Santa Cruz, WNW of San Pedro Pt.

Depth Range: 20-60ft (6-18m)

Access: Boat

Expertise Rating: Novice

ANDREW SALLMON

A golden gorgonian and sea star add to Scorpion's charm.

whitefish and sand bass. Then look for the unexpected. In mid-water, schools of baitfish skitter through the bay, attracting predatory mackerel and yellowtail.

In the calm, deeper water of the harbor mouth, visibility may exceed 50ft. From 20ft above the sand you can survey a wide amphitheater as you search the bottom. Unless there's a plankton bloom, a ripping current or screaming northeast wind, Scorpion's also is a good snorkeling site and a good place for novice divers.

12 Ruby Rock

On the west end of the front side of Santa Cruz, there are perhaps a dozen small coves: among them, Del Mar Caves, Ruby Rock, Painted Cave, Profile Point and Quail Rock. Only diveable when the current is down, each cove features at least one 70ft wall dive, a shallow inshore reef and/or an islet, as well as a sea cave.

At Ruby Rock Cove's western point the wall plummets from just beneath the surface to about 110ft. This is one of the coldest sites on Santa Cruz, especially if you dive deep here. Though "warm" June temperatures can be as cold as 50°F, the panoramic view is worth it. The macrophotography opportunities are also good, including anemones, scallops, cup corals and gorgonians.

The descent at the eastern entrance is more gradual, a series of pebbly ledges from about 40 to 80ft. Calico bass, sheephead and opaleye perch inhabit this region.

In the mouth of the cove and surrounded by muddy sand, a mesa-like structure, perhaps 60ft wide with 10 to 20ft walls in some areas, sits at about 120ft. Look for rockfish and lingcod here, and halibut and rays on the sand.

Ruby Rock rises high above the surface near the beach on the eastern side of the cove. Between the rock and the beach is a narrow kelpy channel. This can be a lovely

Location: Front side of Santa Cruz, NE of West Pt.

Depth Range: 20-130ft (6-40m)

Access: Boat

Expertise Rating: Advanced

shallow dive if the surge isn't churning too hard.

There is a sea cave in the back of the cove. Stay out of it! Without proper gear and training, it's easy to get lost or trapped in a sea cave. Sea lions use many of the sea caves of Santa Cruz as haulout, pupping and nursery areas. If you stumble into a sea lion nursery, you risk a nasty, well-deserved bite.

KATHY DEWET-OLESON
Halibut change coloring to match the sandy bottom.

Santa Rosa Island Dive Sites

Fifteen miles (24km) long and 9 miles (14km) wide, Santa Rosa is the second-largest of the North Channel Islands. Pounded by wind and swell much of the year, Santa Rosa is not known for sightseeing. Nonetheless, the island attracts a lot of divers—mostly lobster-grabbers during the winter and halibut hunters in summer.

The underwater topography of the eastern half of the island, from the northern Carrington Point to the southern Johnson's Lee, is characterized by sandy expanses that are occasionally broken by low reefs or clumps of boulders. Carrington Point, Becher's Bay and Skunk Point are spawning sites for large halibut.

On the northwest side of the island in the warmish water (55 to 65°F, or 13 to 18°C) of Talcott Shoals, bug hunters scramble for 6lb (3kg) lobsters from October through March.

Egg Rock, right in the middle of the San Miguel Passage, is the most spectacular pinnacle in the area, but the current usually precludes diving there. If your boat anchors on this ovoid seamount, consider yourself one of the fortunate few.

When a boat bound for San Miguel or Talcott runs into 10ft (3m) waves in the San Miguel Passage, it may be forced to seek shelter in Johnson's Lee, a sandy bay with a large, kelpy inshore reef on Santa Rosa's south shore. Though it is nobody's first choice, Johnson's Lee is not without its secret charms.

The prettiest dives on Santa Rosa are west of Johnson's Lee on the southwest face and, therefore, often inaccessible due to rough weather. They include South Point, a lovely shallow to midrange inshore reef; Cluster Point, which has an inshore reef similar to the one at South Point and two offshore seamounts that rival those at San Miguel; and Bee Rock, which also features a pinnacle and a shallow reef. Completely exposed to the weather, Bee Rock is visited least.

BONNIE CARDONE

Dusk descends on a dive boat anchored at Johnson's Lee.

With depths exceeding 600ft (180m) only 2 or 3 miles (3 to 5km) to the south, and with constant winds moving the surface water, Santa Rosa's southern sites can be chilly. If you're taking photos, you'd best wear a drysuit. But the cold water (50 to 55°F, or 32 to 41°C) has its upside. Along southern Santa Rosa, species like vermilion rockfish and lingcod, which normally live in deeper water, are common at midrange depths, and the water is sometimes clearer than elsewhere on the island.

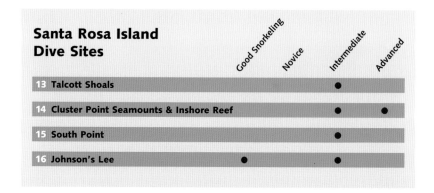

Santa Rosa Island Dive Sites

	Good Snorkeling	Novice	Intermediate	Advanced
13 Talcott Shoals			●	
14 Cluster Point Seamounts & Inshore Reef			●	●
15 South Point			●	
16 Johnson's Lee	●		●	

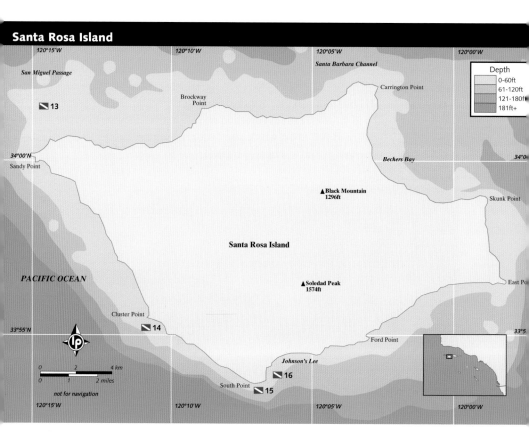

Santa Rosa Island

13 | Talcott Shoals

In fall and winter almost any boat headed for Santa Rosa will make a stop at Talcott Shoals, on the northwest side of the island. Many spend the entire day in its broad, rocky shallows. Once a vast kelp forest, Talcott Shoals has been mostly reduced to urchin barrens, probably by winter storms and recent El Niño conditions.

Location: NW end of Santa Rosa, about 2 miles (3.2km) N of Sandy Pt.

Depth Range: 20-90ft (6-27m)

Access: Boat

Expertise Rating: Intermediate

A series of shallow ledges, running mostly north-south, provides the only shelter for a thriving lobster population. Unlike most lobster habitat, many of these ledges lack back doors opening into deep recesses. At Talcott, a lobster seen is very often a lobster taken. And they grow big. Four- to six-pounders are common.

Despite the absence of kelp, the shoals support an abundance of marine life. Look for copper, grass and vermilion rockfish below 80ft. Olive rockfish hang in the middle depths. Sheephead, calico bass and opaleye inhabit the shallows, especially around the high spot known as **Little Wilson.**

Possibly because the terrain is so wide-open, it's easy to spot nudibranchs— Spanish shawls, sea lemons and aeolids, among others. Sponges, anemones, scallops and sea stars provide countless opportunities for macrophotography.

ANDREW SALLMON

Sunflower sea stars can grow up to 3ft (.9m) in diameter.

14   Cluster Point Seamounts & Inshore Reef

A pair of seamounts, **Rainbow Reef** and **Marty's Reef**, lie about a mile apart, just west of the midpoint between Cluster Point and South Point. Surrounded by at least 120ft of water, neither one rises past about 60ft below the surface.

Location: Back side of Santa Rosa, 4 miles (6.4km) W of South Pt.

Depth Range: 30-120ft (9.1-37m)

Access: Boat

Expertise Rating: Intermediate (inshore reef), Advanced (seamounts)

Bits of wreckage from the *Chickasaw*, a freighter that ran aground at Cluster Point in 1962, still litter both seamounts. On Marty's Reef, the farther east of the two, you may still find a twisted metal ship's ladder wedged firmly into a vertical crack. It looks like it was installed there to help divers climb up and down the pinnacle.

Because visibility in the upper water column is usually limited (clearing below the thermocline) and the current may be somewhat stiff, you must follow the anchor line all the way to the reef. Above the rocks and around the anchor, large schools of blue rockfish nibble at the worms that get stirred up when a boat drops the hook.

The deeper areas of both reefs attract large numbers of vermilion rockfish and lingcod. The rocks are covered with anemones, sponges and large scallops. No matter what the topside weather, these depths are usually calm, silent and serenely beautiful.

The inshore reef begins at Cluster Point and runs more than a mile southeast toward South Point. It's a gorgeous rocky jumble, so similar to the reef at South Point that you would be hard-pressed to know which one you were diving on if the captain didn't tell you. If you dive them both in the same day, you'll probably dive Cluster Point first, and it will likely be a bit rougher and murkier. Otherwise, conditions and marine life are virtually the same.

Farther northwest you'll find a pinnacle that breaks the surface at **Bee Rock**, as well as a kelpy reef on the opposite shoreline. People who've dived them say they're the best dive sites on the island, but maybe that's because the weather often conspires against diving there.

ANDREW SALLMON

Male lingcod will vigilantly guard their nests.

15 South Point

When most outer-island sites are inaccessible or churned up due to rough weather, boats often anchor at South Point, which lies midway between Cluster Point and Ford Point on the back side of Santa Rosa.

At the east end of this mile-long, hundred-yard wide maze of boulders, ledges, tunnels and small caves, a steep 20 to 30ft wall rises from the sand to about 50ft. From there the reef gradually rises toward the shoreline. Divers follow the anchor line to the edge of the wall, while the boat waits over the 80ft-deep sandy bottom. For a change of scenery on subsequent dives, the boat may move a short distance west.

A stiff current often runs outside, and the surge can be strong near the rocky beach, but the middle depths are usually calm enough for intermediate divers to safely explore the endless nooks and crannies and lush kelp stands of this colorful reef. Visibility may extend to 50ft; more often, it's between 10 and 30ft.

Possibly due to the cold water (rarely above 55°F), copper and vermilion rockfish and lingcod are abundant here. Look for them, as well as sheephead and calico bass in the myriad small caves and narrow channels. Olive rockfish hang out in the kelp in mid-water. Scallops, nudibranchs, sponges and anemones decorate the rocks. Once common, a few red abalone may still be found here.

Location: Back side of Santa Rosa, 4 miles (6.4km) WSW of Ford Pt., 4 miles (6.4km) SE of Cluster Pt.

Depth Range: 30-80ft (9.1-24m)

Access: Boat

Expertise Rating: Intermediate

ANDREW SALLMON
South Point's currents feed the red and gold gorgonians.

16 Johnson's Lee

Very few dive charters leave Ventura or Santa Barbara with the idea of spending a day at Johnson's Lee. Nonetheless, when the Point Conception weather buoy reports 12ft waves and 40knot winds, many boats headed to San Miguel wind up here. Especially in winter and spring, you can't always go where you want to.

Location: Back side of Santa Rosa, E of South Pt.

Depth Range: 30-80ft (9.1-24m)

Access: Boat

Expertise Rating: Intermediate

So, you're stuck in Johnson's Lee, disappointed and perhaps a little green around the gills. Make the best of it! Relax, take a few long swims to nowhere in particular. It may not be pretty, but there's some interesting stuff here.

Blue-water hunters love Johnson's Lee because white sea bass feed and spawn here. Croakers, not true bass, whites grow to about 5ft and 80lbs. You'll almost never get near this elusive game fish on scuba. Put away your tank, BC and regulator and grab your snorkel. Creep into a large patch of kelp, hang motionless and wait. If you're lucky, you may see one of these beautiful animals sleeping under the canopy. You may suddenly find yourself in the center of a school of 50 or more. It may last no more than 10 seconds, but it's a peak experience.

Bubbles don't bother schooling pelagics like barracuda, yellowtail and mackerel, drawn to Johnson's Lee by large concentrations of baitfish. If you find a bait ball, stay with it for a while. You never know what kind of critter it will attract.

Sea lions and harbor seals also hunt for food throughout the bay. Squid spawn on the wide stretches of open sand. Wherever you find sand and squid, you may find halibut, especially in summer.

Large, territorial calico bass haunt the small kelp stands around the clumps of boulders in the middle of the bay. Search diligently amid the rocks and you will find a few red abalone. Inshore, calicos dart from cover as you approach, opaleye and garibaldi ride the surge, and telltale antennae betray the presence of lobsters in the rocks.

ANDREW SALLMON

A diver explores one of Johnson Lee's kelp stands.

San Miguel Island Dive Sites

The westernmost of the North Channel Islands, San Miguel is 45 miles (72km) west of Santa Barbara Harbor and more than 60 miles (95km) west of Ventura. Santa Barbara boats leave at 2am; Ventura boats, at midnight. Due to cold water, mediocre visibility in many areas, currents and surge, San Miguel dive sites are all rated intermediate or advanced.

The island is only 9 miles (14km) long, and is 4 miles (6.4km) wide at its midpoint. San Miguel falls outside the lee of Point Conception, so be prepared for a rough ride if there's a big swell from the north. Sometimes it's too rough to dive the world-class sites on the front (north) side. Sometimes boats can't even make it to San Miguel and must seek shelter on the lee side of Santa Rosa or Santa Cruz. In that case, no matter how much you want to get to Miguel, you'll bless the captain for turning back.

Its relative inaccessibility has helped San Miguel remain utterly wild and nearly pristine. Compared to the inner islands, San Miguel's fish and invertebrate species, with the exception of abalone, have not suffered from overharvesting and environmental degradation. To experience this abundance, divers pay more, risk disappointment and often endure one helluva bumpy ride.

In good weather you will likely begin your four-dive day at one of four spectacular front-side seamounts, followed by a series of progressively shallower dives on scenic front-side reefs. The back side offers less variety than the front, but can still be quite pleasant and worthwhile. If you stay awake on the way home, you may see porpoises, Risso's dolphins, orcas and, in summer, humpback and blue whales.

Several pinniped rookeries (including two large northern elephant seal colonies as well as sea lions, northern fur seals, harbor seals and, occasionally, Steller sea lions) fall within the San Miguel Ecological Reserve, a 5-mile (8km) strip of shore running around the west end of the island. To protect these animals and nesting sea birds, boats may not approach closer than 300 yards (275m) offshore. Elsewhere on San Miguel, from March 15 through April 30 and from October 1 through December 15, the boating proximity limit is 100 yards (90m). No special Fish and Game restrictions apply within this reserve. You rarely dive at San Miguel without a sea lion escort.

ANDREW SALLMON

Pinnipeds have colonized San Miguel's west end.

This abundance of pinnipeds attracts predatory great white sharks, which are known to hunt at the west end of San Miguel. A few scuba divers have encountered white sharks in this area, but there have been no verified white shark attacks on scuba divers in Southern California.

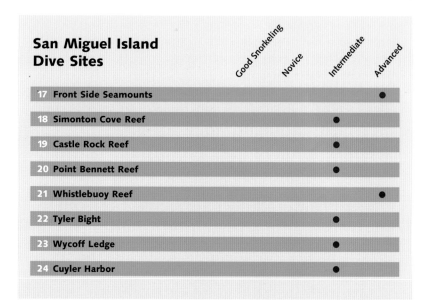

San Miguel Island Dive Sites	Good Snorkeling	Novice	Intermediate	Advanced
17 Front Side Seamounts				●
18 Simonton Cove Reef			●	
19 Castle Rock Reef			●	
20 Point Bennett Reef			●	
21 Whistlebuoy Reef				●
22 Tyler Bight			●	
23 Wycoff Ledge			●	
24 Cuyler Harbor			●	

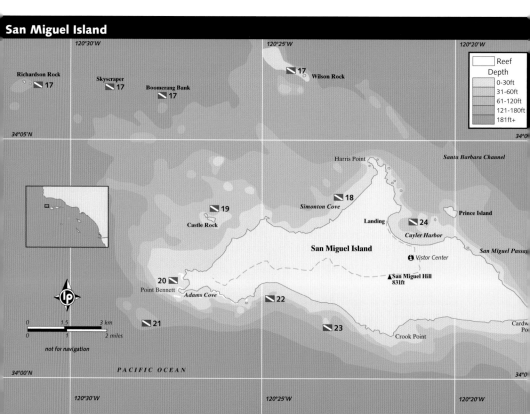

17   Front Side Seamounts

Weather permitting, a dive trip to San Miguel begins with a stop at one of the front-side seamounts. Although the topography at each of these sites is distinctive, they present similar challenges and sightseeing opportunities.

At the eastern end of a 7-mile chain, **Wilson Rock** lies about 4 miles north of Simonton Cove. **Boomerang Bank** is 6 miles north of Point Bennett. **Richardson Rock** is 7 miles northwest of Point Bennett. **Skyscraper** is between Boomerang and Richardson.

Wilson, closest to the island and protected from the south swell in summer, has been hard hit by sport divers harvesting scallops. A smaller reef, Skyscraper is visited less than Wilson and has suffered less diver-related damage. A stiff current flows through a sandy channel cut through the middle of Boomerang, but it largely dies away when you reach the deep, moat-like regions of the inner structure. From one side Richardson is reminiscent of an old-fashioned rolltop desk.

As you descend upon any of these, the view is quite spectacular: Sheer walls plunge through dark blue water to meet the sand at around 200ft. White, strawberry and green anemones, cobalt and orange sponges, tunicates, sea stars, mussels, scallops, tube worms and sea urchins colonize every inch of surface area. Brittle stars, nudibranchs, crabs and snails crawl through the maze of invertebrate life.

Blue and olive rockfish school in the middle depths, while garibaldi and surfperch ride the surge. Below 100ft the reefs provide shelter from the swell and the water is normally very calm and clear. In this silent, peaceful space you'll find china, gopher, copper and vermilion

Location: 4 sites, 4-7 miles (6.4-11km) N to NW of San Miguel

Depth Range: 60-130ft (18-40m)

Access: Boat

Expertise Rating: Advanced

rockfish, lingcod and an occasional wolf eel. Bring a light to see their true colors.

The tops of Boomerang and Skyscraper are between 60 and 90ft below the surface, depending on the tide. Richardson and Wilson Rocks rise a few feet above the water, surrounded by churning boilers. On a foggy morning, jumping off a rolling deck in the middle of nowhere requires some gumption. If you are not a strong swimmer or a skillful underwater navigator, these dives are not for you.

If there is a plankton bloom above the thermocline, you must follow the anchor line all the way to the reef, or you may become disoriented and miss it entirely. Dive up-current from the anchor. Closely monitor your depth and bottom time. If possible, use the anchor line to ascend and make a safety stop.

Encrusting sponges camouflage decorator crabs.

BONNIE CARDONE

18 Simonton Cove Reef

Covered with a dense kelp canopy, this mile of rocky, mound-like reef is cut by a quarter-mile sand channel and runs parallel to the shoreline of Simonton Cove. All sides of the reef slope gently down to a white-sand bottom.

Unless the northwest swell is pounding, the cove is a calm and pleasant place to dive. Simonton is one of the few places on San Miguel where a new diver may enjoy a long, aimless excursion in relatively clear, shallow water. Navigation is simple, but it's important to save enough air to return under the kelp. Anytime you dive the west end of Miguel, it is prudent to avoid long surface swims.

On a sunny day the reef is a sightseer's delight. Olive rockfish and calico bass lurk amid the kelp fronds, waiting to ambush unwary baitfish. Gopher and china rockfish, cabezon and lingcod hide amid the rocks. Schools of brine shrimp, anchovies and krill form bait balls in mid-water.

Location: About ¼ mile (.4km) offshore, N of the military marker in Simonton Cove

Depth Range: 30-60ft (9.1-18m)

Access: Boat

Expertise Rating: Intermediate

You may see dogfish, harmless grey smoothhound sharks and electric rays in Simonton. Sea lions and harbor seals are common here. In spring and fall, northern elephant seals colonize the far west end of the cove. You can easily observe their activities from the deck of the boat.

This reef still supports a thriving population of red abalone. (In 1997, with all abalone species facing extinction in Southern California due to overharvesting and disease, the Department of Fish and Game closed the abalone fishery south of San Francisco.) At Crook Point, on the back side of Miguel, there is an even healthier red ab colony. Since the department has given no sign of reopening the fishery, there is every reason to hope that the snails will recolonize the entire island.

In summer, 30 to 50lb California halibut enter the cove to spawn. Local spearfishermen book passage to San Miguel in hopes of getting one of these magnificent fish. If you are uncomfortable around this kind of activity, it would be best to ask the charter operator if the boat allows spearfishing.

BONNIE CARDONE
Red abalone thrive along Simonton Cove Reef.

19 Castle Rock Reef

A jumble of boulders, rocky mounds, sand channels and short walls, the reef around Castle Rock is more than 3 miles wide from east to west. Less than half a mile of open water, rarely deeper than 100ft, separates the southwest border of Castle Rock Reef from Point Bennett Reef, at the western extremity of the island.

Location: Front side of San Miguel, 1½ miles (2.4km) NE of Pt. Bennett

Depth Range: 30-80ft (9.1-24m)

Access: Boat

Expertise Rating: Intermediate

For practical purposes, it's pretty hard to say where one reef ends and the other begins. You can dive just about anywhere you like on the west end of San Miguel, provided you can anchor safely. Above 30ft the surge can be quite strong.

You can find something interesting almost anywhere on this thoroughly enjoyable reef. Copper and vermilion rockfish, lingcod and cabezon hide in the cracks and crevices. Anemones, sea stars and nudibranchs decorate the rocks. Electric rays hover in mid-water. Kelp flourishes wherever the water is less than about 60ft deep. There's a sea lion haul-out on Castle Rock and a large rookery at Point Bennett, so you're unlikely to dive without a pinniped escort.

Until the abalone fishery was closed in 1997, this area was a favorite spot for commercial and recreational red abalone harvesters. In the '90s the Castle Rock abalone population suffered greatly from overharvesting and disease. These rocks, once covered with snails, now bear the scars that mark where abalone used to cling.

BONNIE CARDONE

Castle Rock is teaming with macro life.

20 Point Bennett Reef

The west end of San Miguel Island is a true wilderness, home to some of the most amazing creatures on earth. Falling within the San Miguel Ecological Reserve and ringed by a maze of treacherous shoals, the inshore waters from Adams Cove on the south to Point Bennett Reef on the north remain relatively untouched.

Location: West end of San Miguel

Depth Range: 30-80ft (9.1-24m)

Access: Boat

Expertise Rating: Intermediate

For a dive boat to navigate safely here, the conditions must be mild. Boats usually anchor over a wall that rises to about 30ft from a rocky bottom at about 70ft. The water is rarely warmer than 55°F, except in late summer, when it may reach 65°F. Horizontal visibility often extends to 50ft, but it can be soupy above the thermocline.

The rocks are alive with invertebrates, and the water teems with large vermilion rockfish and other *Sebastes* species. Vermilions grow slowly—a 10-pounder may be 40 years old. So far, Point Bennett

BONNIE CARDONE
Juvenile sea lions often cavort with divers.

has not been subjected to the kind of repetitive sportfishing and spearfishing pressure that has stripped other reefs of mature individuals.

This reef offers a wide variety of macrophotography subjects and, if the water is clear, a chance for wide-angle shots of sea lions and reef fish. On a sunny day the reef sparkles with light and color. A protracted, shallow dive in the amber kelp can be a sightseer's delight.

Bring binoculars—elephant seals haul out at Adams Cove in the spring and fall. In-water elephant seal encounters are very rare, but observing them on the beach is fascinating. It is unusual, on the other hand, to dive here without meeting sea lions from the Point Bennett rookery. Use caution around these animals. Females and juveniles, often delightfully playful and curious, are sometimes downright hostile. Adult males are almost always aggressive.

Great white sharks prey upon elephant seals and sea lions. Although white shark sightings are extremely rare, one probably killed a commercial urchin diver near Point Bennett in 1994. Avoid long surface swims.

21 Whistlebuoy Reef

Whistlebuoy Reef, a smallish seamount, is completely exposed to every swell and wind. Consequently, crosscurrents are common—the wind may blow you one way while the deep current is running in another direction.

Even at great depth, a tremendous surge may roll through the reef, tossing divers about like game pieces. Because of the challenges it presents, most boats will only visit this site on a dead-calm, perfect day.

Location: About ½ mile (.8km) SW of Pt. Bennett

Depth Range: 60-130ft (18-40m)v

Access: Boat

Expertise Rating: Advanced

Horizontal visibility above the thermocline (at 50 to 70ft) may be less than 20ft due to plankton bloom. Below the bloom, visibility will usually clear to 50ft or more. If you miss the reef, you risk descending well beyond the sport-diving limit.

It's imperative to descend the anchor line to the reef and navigate back to the anchor at the end of the dive. By ascending the anchor line, you can easily make safety stops and avoid being swept away from the boat by the surface current.

The reef is an amazing structure, like a castle wall with turrets and parapets. One feels like an astronaut, descending upon the ruins of a lost civilization on an unknown planet. Depending on the tide, the top may be as deep as 90ft or as shallow as 60ft. There is a steep, 30ft drop-off on the inside of the wall.

Like most deep North Channel seamounts, Whistle-buoy Reef is completely encrusted with colorful invertebrate life: scallops, nudibranchs and sea stars, as well as metridium, straw-

berry and green anemones. No kelp grows at this depth, but the reef provides shelter for a healthy population of rock-fish, cabezon and lingcod.

If the wind is right, the water may be soupy with jellyfish. In the warmer months you may see mola-molas feeding here. During El Niño years, turtles have been seen grazing on jellies off the west end of San Miguel.

BONNIE CARDONE

A sea star adds a splash of color to this small seamount.

22　Tyler Bight

When a pounding north swell or fierce winds off the high desert create unsafe conditions on the front side of San Miguel, dive boats retreat to the shelter of the back side. If the swell is not completely wrapped around the west end, the captain may decide to anchor in the lee of Tyler Bight.

The reef, a series of rock piles, boulders and low walls running more or less parallel to the island for about a mile, is marked by dense kelp. Divers may choose

Location: Back side of San Miguel, 2-3 miles (3-5km) E of Pt. Bennett

Depth Range: 30-80ft (9.1-24m)

Access: Boat

Expertise Rating: Intermediate

to head south where the rocks meet the sand at 70 to 90ft, explore the midrange

depths around the boat, or navigate north for a shallow dive.

While not particularly picturesque, Tyler is not without its charms. Search the boulders and kelp holdfasts for sea hares and their yellow or pink fibrous egg masses. Working your way over the sand, you may see ocean whitefish feeding on squid eggs, or diving cormorants poking in the sand for worms and snails. Look under ledges for lingcod resting after a meal of squid. Copper and vermilion rockfish hide from marauding sea lions amid the deeper rocks.

Sea hares lay spaghetti-like piles of eggs.

23 Wycoff Ledge

Wycoff Ledge is about the prettiest spot on the south side of San Miguel. Smack dab in the center of the island, it's usually the calmest, clearest and warmest site as well. There's a steep, 30ft drop-off on the eastern end of the half-mile reef, and much of the structure is riddled with small caves, archways and channels.

Illuminated by sunlight filtering through the amber kelp, an abundance of coralline red algae, sponges, scallops, nudibranchs and anemones bedeck the rocks. On a clear day Wycoff Ledge is an excellent place for macrophotography.

Although Wycoff Ledge is not a prime game site, you'll find cabezon, rockfish and the occasional large sheephead or calico bass in the holes. In the shallow areas and in mid-water there's the usual aggregation of senorita wrasses, garibaldi, topsmelt, surfperch and opaleye.

Location: Back side of San Miguel, S of military marker

Depth Range: 30-80ft (9.1-24m)

Access: Boat

Expertise Rating: Intermediate

Harbor seals like to hunt along this well-stocked reef. One of these round-bellied, curious pinnipeds is likely to observe you closely at some point during your dive.

There used to be quite a few red abalone here. Probably because the area has been dived so heavily for so long, abs are now scarce around Wycoff Ledge. At Crook Point, 2 miles to the east, the snails are still abundant.

24 Cuyler Harbor

Sheltered by Harris Point to the northwest and the main body of the island to the south, Cuyler Harbor often has the calmest and warmest water on San Miguel. An expansive, intricate sunlit reef system, clear water and lots of fish make this shallow little bay an ideal spot for a relaxing, final dive of the day.

Calico bass, sand bass, garibaldi, sheephead, cabezon and rockfish inhabit the reefs. In the center of the harbor, some of the reefs make boilers where they rise nearly to the surface. Unless you want to get tossed around, avoid these. In the sandy areas between the rocks you'll find bat rays, schools of baitfish, brine shrimp and krill.

In summer, California halibut, which may grow to 5ft long and weigh as much as 70lbs, enter the shallows to spawn. Large as they are, these fish aren't easy to spot. Halibut hunt squid and baitfish at night and rest during the day. Before settling down to sleep, they thoroughly cover themselves with sand, often leav-

Location: Front side of San Miguel, 1-2 miles (1.5-3km) southeast of Harris Pt.

Depth Range: 30-60ft (9.1-18m)

Access: Boat

Expertise Rating: Intermediate

ing no more than a pair of eyes, or the vague outline of a mouth or tail, above the sand. You'll probably swim over ten for every one you see.

Perhaps 100 yards wide, **Prince Island** sits in the northeast entrance to the harbor. If the current is not too stiff, boats sometimes anchor between Prince Island and Cuyler Harbor's outer reef. You may see blue sharks cruising in mid-water in this little channel. Below 60ft or so, the rocks around Prince Island are a good place to look for large specimens of lingcod, vermilion rockfish and cabezon.

Calm Cuyler Harbor is an ideal spot for the day's final dive.

North Channel
Shore Dive Sites

Refugio State Beach

Coastal geography and marine weather patterns determine beach diving conditions along the North Channel shore. As a rule, storms come from the north in winter and spring and from the south in summer and fall—but don't plan your dives based on this generalization. Sometimes there are simultaneous storms off Mexico and Alaska. Sometimes the weather comes straight out of the west. The best way to choose a shore dive is to check the weather, wind and swell conditions and look carefully at the site's coastal orientation. (See page 41 for a sample swell model.)

From Point Arguello (at the northwestern tip of the Bight of California) south to Santa Monica Bay, the coastline runs roughly west to east except for a short north-south stretch between Ventura and Oxnard.

Near Santa Barbara, Refugio State Beach and Mohawk Reef are partially protected from a north swell by Point Conception. The Channel Islands also shield

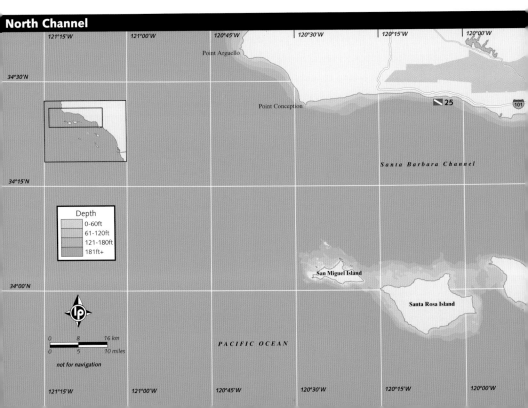

these sites from southern weather. Deer Creek Road and County Line (between Ventura and Santa Monica) are open to the south, but are fairly well protected from northern waves. Palos Verdes Peninsula shields the southern half of Santa Monica Bay and Malaga Cove from the south swell, but not from northerly Pacific storms.

While many North Cannel shore dive sites make for a rewarding day of diving, they can also be difficult or even dangerous under the wrong conditions. Doing some research beforehand definitely pays off.

North Channel Shore Dive Sites	Good Snorkeling	Novice	Intermediate	Advanced
25 Refugio State Beach	●		●	
26 Mohawk Reef	●		●	
27 Deer Creek Road	●		●	
28 County Line Beach	●		●	
29 Malaga Cove	●		●	

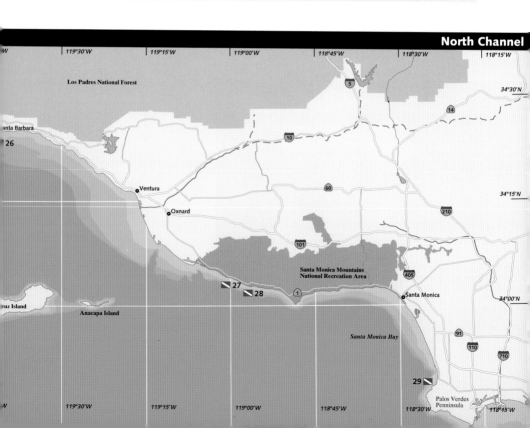

25 Refugio State Beach

Highway 101 follows the coastline west out of Santa Barbara for about 30 miles before turning north at Gaviota toward San Luis Obispo. **Tajiguas** and Refugio State Beach, two nearly adjacent sites about 20 miles west of Santa Barbara, both offer divers easy access to shallow, kelpy inshore reefs.

Location: About 20 miles (32km) W of Santa Barbara on Hwy 101

Depth Range: 15-30ft (4.6-9.1m)

Access: Shore

Expertise Rating: Intermediate

It costs nothing to dive at Tajiguas, an undeveloped site. At Refugio State Beach, parking costs $6 per day, and public showers, toilets and phones are available. In the summer, with a lifeguard on duty and a snack shack serving burgers, Refugio is the better bargain. The highway exit is clearly marked.

For whatever reason, the inshore reefs at Tajiguas are not as "fishy" as the ones at Refugio, but the rocks are covered with invertebrate photo subjects like anemones and nudibranchs. If you're not a photographer, your best bet is free-diving at Refugio. As is often the case at beach or inner-island sites, the fish are easily spooked by bubbles. Your chances of seeing calico bass, opaleye or sheephead improve greatly if you're free-diving.

There are two reefs at Refugio, one at each end of the cove, both within swimming distance of the wide, flat, sandy beach. Rarely deeper than 20ft, the eastern reef is only 50 yards out. It's a pretty little reef, with kelp, senoritas, nudibranchs, sea hares, sponges, sea stars and anemones.

The western reef is quite a bit farther from the shore, past the breakers at the western entrance to the cove. Getting there should be no problem if you're snorkeling, but the trek is potentially tiring on scuba. In winter or spring, if you swim out in the early morning, you may catch a glimpse of white sea bass snaking their way through the kelp.

Refugio has more than a hundred campsites. To reserve one, or to obtain more information, call ☎ (800) 444-7275 or visit the state park website at www .cal-parks.ca.gov.

ANDREW SALLMON

Sea lemons are one of Southern California's most commonly seen nudibranchs.

26 | Mohawk Reef

Sheltered by South Point, Mohawk Reef runs parallel to the shoreline from Arroyo Burro County Park to within about a mile of Santa Barbara Harbor's western breakwater. With a variety of interesting structures, clear water and a large kelp forest, Mohawk may be the best beach dive in the area, but it's not the easiest.

Location: Just west of Santa Barbara Harbor, off Cliff Dr.

Depth Range: 15-40ft (4.6-12m)

Access: Shore

Expertise Rating: Intermediate

From the harbor, take Shoreline Drive west. Turn left onto Cliff Drive and park at Mesa Lane or Arroyo Burro (both are left turns off Cliff Drive). At Arroyo Burro you've got a long walk east along the beach before your entry. At Mesa Lane the reef is right in front of you and a bit more sheltered, but first you must descend the infamous "Thousand Steps," a sturdy wooden staircase from the street down the cliff to the beach. At the end of your dive you must, obviously, ascend them.

For this reason, snorkeling may be a better option than scuba diving at Mohawk Reef. For snorkelers, Mesa Lane is clearly the better entry point. If you insist on waddling down the beach in full scuba gear, go in at Arroyo Burro.

At Mesa Lane the reef begins less than 50 yards offshore. In the eelgrass between the reef and the beach, look for rubberlip surfperch, senoritas and pipefish. The reef is home to cabezon, swell sharks and rockfish. Many harbor seals haul out nearby—one may even decide to join you.

As you enter the kelp, look for baitfish, calico bass, sheephead and opaleye. On the outside, where the reef drops down to 40ft, you may see lingcod and the occasional lobster.

Around Mohawk you can see a rare type of *macrocystis* (giant kelp). This subspecies or new species (scientists do not agree) has developed a unique holdfast that allows it to grow in sand. Other types of kelp require a rocky substrate.

Giant kelp is composed of a stemlike stipe, gas-filled pneumatocysts and leaflike blades.

27 Deer Creek Road

Southeast of Point Mugu, Highway 1 hugs the coastline. At the intersection of Deer Creek Road and the highway, the water is a stone's throw from the pavement. A short wooden stairway leads to a tiny beach, and a healthy reef lies just offshore. If the swell is down, this can be Southern California's easiest worthwhile shore dive.

Location: SE Ventura County; intersection of Hwy 1 and Deer Creek Rd.

Depth Range: 15-40ft (4.6-12m)

Access: Shore

Expertise Rating: Intermediate

The reef system, three sections marked by three kelp stands, begins at a depth of 20ft about 50ft offshore. The reef extends for close to 200 yards along the beach and nearly the same distance into the channel. Even in calm weather, visibility may be limited in the shallows, but it's usually better on the outside.

The easiest entry/exit area is near the stairs. Begin your dive by swimming up-current, especially if you're on scuba; you don't want to find yourself a hundred yards down-current of the stairs, weary and low on air, with an up-current swim to get to your exit point. Fortunately, at Deer Creek you've got shelter from the current (thick kelp and a complex reef) within a few yards of shore.

The current may be hard on divers, but it carries plankton, krill and brine shrimp—baitfish eat that stuff, and game fish eat baitfish. You'll find calico bass, sheephead and opaleye over the reef; lingcod, rockfish and a few lobsters in the rocks; and halibut and rays in the sand. Scallops, sponges and nudibranchs provide dabs of color. Yellowtail sometimes chase baitfish on the outside.

Spearfishermen like this spot for halibut in summer and white sea bass in winter. Parking on the southbound side of the road is limited, so get there early. There are no facilities.

28 County Line Beach

County Line Beach and **Leo Carrillo State Beach** straddle Ventura and Los Angeles counties. Both sites are better known as surfing (and windsurfing, at Carrillo) spots than as dive sites. If you don't believe it, dust off your Beach Boys records.

Leo Carrillo offers all the advantages of a state beach: showers, lifeguards, safe parking and chow. The reef is also quite close to the beach—another plus. Clubs and classes often use this park. But the best diving areas are also near the best

Location: SE Ventura County; intersection of Hwy 1 and Yerba Buena Rd.

Depth Range: 15-40ft (4.6-12m)

Access: Shore

Expertise Rating: Intermediate

surf breaks and are likely to be completely overrun with surfers.

County Line, also known as Harrison's Reef, is a long swim, at least 200 yards, but worth it. For one thing, it's well outside the surf line. For the shortest swim, park on the ocean side of Highway 1, past Neptune's Net (a restaurant) and as close to the east end of the beach as you can get.

At some points the kelp patch is more than 100 yards wide. If you're scuba diving, save enough air to traverse the kelp underwater at the end of your dive.

A famous local fishing hole, Harrison's is probably the healthiest inshore reef in the North Channel. The marine life is quite similar to what you'll find at Deer Creek Road, except there are more lobsters in the rock piles, more halibut in the sand, more bass in the kelp, more invertebrates, more of everything, espe-

cially on the outside. There's also a lot more reef, at least a mile of it. If it wasn't such a long swim, it would be perfect.

ANDREW SALLMON

Look for Norris's top snails on the kelp fronds at County Line.

29 Malaga Cove

Almost all who get certified in L.A. County do beach dives at **Avenue C**, Redondo Beach. But unless you're hunting halibut or fascinated with garbage, you probably wouldn't choose to dive there.

A few miles south there are several good sites on the side of the Palos Verdes Peninsula facing Santa Monica Bay. Free-divers hunt white sea bass in the kelp at **Flat Rock**, **Rocky Point** and **Bluff Cove**, but it's a long haul down steep, sometimes treacherous paths to these

Location: L.A. County, just west of Torrance Beach

Depth Range: 15-50ft (4.6-15m)

Access: Shore

Expertise Rating: Intermediate

rocky beaches. Up the cliff in scuba gear? Forget about it!

Malaga Cove offers the easiest access to a decent dive in the southern reaches of Santa Monica Bay. To get there from LAX, take Highway 1 south, turn right onto Palos Verdes Boulevard. After about a mile, turn right onto Via Corta. Via Corta merges with Via Almar. Turn right onto Via Arroyo and continue to the end of the street, where it meets Paseo del Mar. Park on the street or in the school parking lot. A paved path to the beach is just behind the school. If you have a rolling tank caddy, it will work fine here.

At the bottom of the path there's a swimming club to the left of the beach, then a church. **Torrance Beach** (Rat Beach, to the locals), on your right, provides an easy entrance on gradually sloping sand. The medium-depth reef about 150 yards in front of the church offers some rock piles and ledges scattered in the sand.

There is also a wide, shallow reef directly in front of the pool and the church. Avoid this area if you're on scuba. You can get trapped on the shoals, and it's a very difficult exit.

For some reason, swell sharks and horn sharks love this little cove. You can also find bat rays, angel sharks, guitarfish, halibut and large crabs in the sand, and calico bass, senorita wrasses, garibaldi and sheephead over the rocks.

The scenery here is not spectacular, but it's often calm, and the water is warm for these parts. In good weather this can be a long, comfortable dive.

Horn sharks rest quietly on the floor of Malaga Cove.

Santa Catalina Island Dive Sites

Santa Catalina is the largest of the South Channel Islands and is the closest to the mainland. It is also the only Channel Island with a permanent civilian settlement and the only one not owned by some branch of the U.S. government. Catalina is just a short boat ride from San Pedro or Long Beach, and most of the popular front-side sites are usually diveable except in very bad weather. On some summer days a dozen charters and a flotilla of private boats bring divers to Catalina.

The water is warmer and clearer at Catalina than at Santa Barbara, San Nicolas or the North Channel Islands. When a big swell makes a mess of Southern California's mainland beaches, Catalina's front side is often downright placid. Easy access to many beautiful sites has made diving big business on Catalina.

On the front-side reefs, populations of pink and green abalone, now protected, were previously harvested nearly to the point of extinction. Populations of sheephead, easy prey for sport divers, have also suffered, as have calico bass. Within the front-side ecological reserves between the Isthmus and Avalon and on the back side of Catalina, the situation is better.

Avalon, near the east end, is a thriving tourist town with several dive shops and an airfill station on the beach. Several Avalon hotels cater to divers, and a few dive charter boats operate out of Avalon Harbor.

Avalon Underwater Park is probably the busiest shore-diving site in Southern California. Around the island, near designated campsites (available by permit only), you will also find a lot of beach diving activity.

At Two Harbors, the small town on the narrow neck of land between Isthmus Harbor on the front side and Catalina Harbor on the back, there is a dive shop, an airfill station, some licensed dive boats and a state-of-the-art recompression chamber.

Because Catalina is so big and so thoroughly explored, there are many well-known dive sites. This guide includes those sites that are the most popular with local divers and the most likely to be enjoyable for novices or divers new to Southern California waters.

BONNIE CARDONE

Take a walk at the water's edge in Avalon.

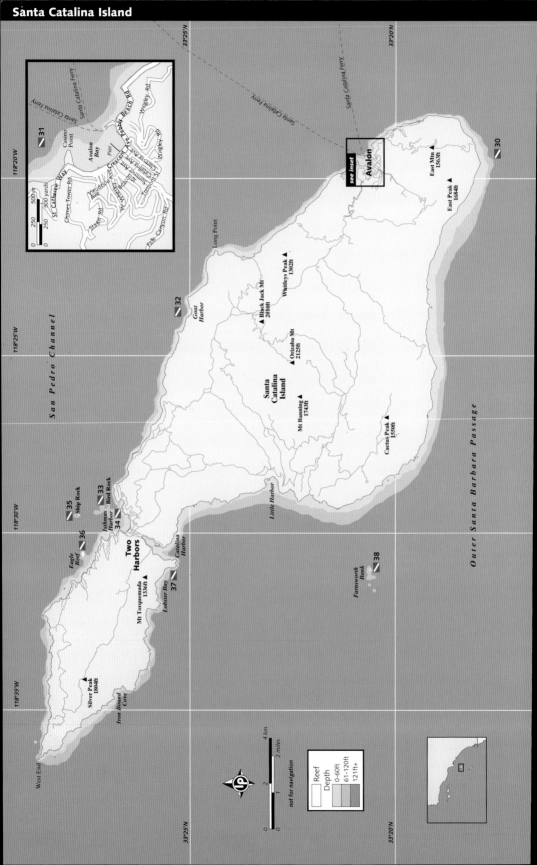

Santa Catalina Island

San Pedro Channel

Outer Santa Barbara Passage

Santa Catalina Ferry

see inset

Avalon

East Mtn 1563ft ▲

East Peak 1684ft ▲

Long Point

Whitleys Peak 1302ft ▲

Black Jack Mt 2010ft ▲

Orizaba Mt 2125ft ▲

Santa Catalina Island

Goat Harbor

Mt Banning 1743ft ▲

Cactus Peak 1500ft ▲

Little Harbor

Ship Rock

Bird Rock

Isthmus Harbor

Two Harbors

Eagle Reef

Catalina Harbor

Mt Torquemada 1336ft ▲

Lobster Bay

Farnsworth Bank

Silver Peak 1804ft ▲

Iron Round Cove

West End

30

31

32

33

34

35

36

37

38

not for navigation

Reef

Depth
0-60ft
61-120ft
121ft+

4 km

2 miles

2

1

Inset — Avalon

Santa Catalina Ferry

Casino Point

Avalon Bay

Pier

Wrigley Rd

Wrigley Rd

Pebble Beach Rd

St Catherine Way

Chimes Tower Rd

Stage Rd

Falls Canyon Rd

Crescent Ave

Sumner Ave

Whittley Ave

Metropole Ave

Clarissa Ave

Beacon St

Tremont St

Catalina Ave

31

250 500ft

250 500 yards

0

0

118°20'W

118°25'W

118°30'W

118°35'W

33°25'N

33°20'N

Santa Catalina Island Dive Sites

	Good Snorkeling	Novice	Intermediate	Advanced
30 Church Rock	●		●	
31 Avalon Underwater Park	●	●		
32 Goat Harbor	●	●	●	
33 Bird Rock	●		●	
34 Isthmus Reef	●	●		
35 Ship Rock	●		●	
36 Eagle Reef	●		●	
37 Cat Head Wall				●
38 Farnsworth Bank				●

30 Church Rock

About 2 miles west of Seal Rocks, Church Rock lies 150 yards off the southern side of the east end of Catalina Island. Exposed to the south and west swells, it is also near the confluence of currents flowing down the outer Santa Barbara Passage and the San Pedro Channel.

Church Rock is often subject to severe current and surge, but on a calm day, especially when Santa Ana conditions prevail, any diver can safely enjoy this beautiful little reef. A smallish site that is a bit out of the way, it's often less crowded than other Catalina dives.

The currents bring nutrients, which stimulate plankton growth. Shrimp and baitfish eat plankton. Predatory schooling fish, like yellowtail and barracuda, follow the bait. The open

Location: SE end of Catalina

Depth Range: 15-60ft (4.6-18m)

Access: Boat

Expertise Rating: Intermediate

BONNIE CARDONE
A golden sunset caps a day of diving at Church Rock.

water outside Church Rock can be an exciting place to snorkel, but you must maintain a constant vigil for boat traffic.

As you approach the site from seaward you'll see long strands of feather boa kelp waving in the surge. Coralline algae, anemones, sponges and nudibranchs decorate the rocks. On a sunny day you'll immediately know why underwater photography classes visit this site.

In the middle of the reef, just below the surface, a ring of boilers surrounds a shallow, sheltered area. This is a magical place, with a few tunnels large enough to crawl through wearing scuba gear. At times the walls of these underwater caves and arches are lined with lobsters. Look for moray eels in the darker holes.

Male sheephead and trophy-sized bull calico bass stake out their territory in the grottoes between the rocks. These wise old fish tend to be very spooky—it is far easier for breath-hold divers than scuba divers to approach them.

31　Avalon Underwater Park

Avalon Underwater Park at Casino Point is a unique Channel Islands site. You can dive the outer area from locally based boats, but most folks enter from the breakwater. A series of steps cut into the rock make this entrance less taxing. There

Location: W breakwater, Avalon Harbor

Depth Range: 20-110ft (6-34m)

Access: Shore

Expertise Rating: Novice

is regular airfill service at the park, and several Avalon hotels will run your gear over to the site for little or no charge.

The park offers a variety of terrain and habitat. A kelp bed, densely populated with calico bass and sheephead, occupies a large area to the east of the point. Near the southeastern border the bottom drops from 50 to about 100ft. Here you can explore the flattened wreck of the *Sue Jac*, a 65ft sailboat.

Straight out from the casino, several rocky formations rise from the sand. This area and the shallow rocks are good for snorkeling. Near the park's northwestern border, at the mouth of **Descanso Bay**, conservationists have sunk several small boats and a pile of

BONNIE CARDONE

Blacksmith school above the rubble bottom.

assorted junk to provide habitat for fish and invertebrates.

Avalon Underwater Park is a highly controlled environment. No fishing, taking of game, or boat traffic are allowed within its roped-off boundaries. Game animals that are heavily fished and hunted in other areas, such as lobsters, sheephead and calico bass, have grown used to divers and are easily approached at this site. **Lover's Cove Reserve,** another "no-take" reserve, is within walking distance of Avalon Underwater Park. It extends 100 yards from the shoreline of the southeast corner of Cabrillo Wharf (in Avalon Harbor) to Ring Rock.

The park's absence of boat traffic, easy access and the availability of airfills make it very attractive to instructors. Any summer weekend the breakwater throngs with advanced and rescue classes.

A short stay in an Avalon hotel and a few splashes in the Underwater Park are an ideal introduction to Southern California diving for novices or divers new to this region.

32   Goat Harbor

Goat Harbor, about 1½ miles west of Long Point on the front side of Catalina, is a calm anchorage with a long, kelpy inshore reef, an eastern wall that descends to more than 100ft and a great free-diving site called **Twin Rocks** at its eastern entrance.

About a half mile offshore, the San Pedro Channel is more than 1,000ft

Location: Front side of Catalina, about 1½ miles (2.4km) W of Long Pt.

Depth Range: 10-110ft (3-34m)

Access: Shore or boat

Expertise Rating: Novice (harbor) Intermediate (Twin Rocks)

A school of garibaldi swims through Goat Harbor's kelpy inshore reef.

deep, so it is not uncommon for squid to spawn here and pelagics to come inshore after them. Snorkelers often see yellowtail and white sea bass in the area around Twin Rocks.

Visibility may exceed 50ft at the surface, farther still below 80ft. In the shallow, inshore area, the water can be as warm as 75°F in the summer. It's usually pretty calm in the harbor, but the current can be quite strong, especially near Twin Rocks.

The deep dive begins in a rocky kelp stand and descends steadily to the floor of the harbor at 110 to 120ft, depending on the tide. Sand bass, sheephead and calico bass flit between the rocks on the sloping wall. In the silence at the bottom, bat rays, sleek angel sharks, unusual guitarfish and well-camouflaged halibut sleep on the sand.

You may find a few pink and green abalone in the amber kelp grotto near the shore. Harbor seals like to hide in the rocks of the shallow western reef, then spring out to ambush baitfish. Schools of yellowtail and barracuda sometimes follow the bait right up to the shore. You can spend all day in Goat Harbor and never be bored.

33 Bird Rock

An ovoid, guano-covered mound, Bird Rock marks the eastern entrance to Isthmus Harbor. The rock and its surrounding reef run for about a quarter mile, from southeast to northwest. Dive charters based in Long Beach, San Pedro, Avalon and the Isthmus all regularly visit Bird Rock.

Baitfish seem to like circling Bird Rock, which makes it an excellent place to snorkel. In summer you might watch cormorants diving on topsmelt, while marauding yellowtail drive the fish into a bait ball. But stay close to the rock to avoid being run over by careless weekend sailors intent on reaching their mooring.

On the channel side Bird Rock drops precipitously away to more than 120ft. With visibility usually better than 50ft, this is a dramatic, beautiful scuba dive. Tall kelp stands grow from large boulders above 60 or 70ft. Deeper, the kelp gives way to gorgonians. Look for large calico bass threading their way through these fan-shaped growths. Big lobsters are also known to inhabit the deeper regions.

Location: Front side of Catalina, NE entrance to Isthmus Harbor

Depth Range: 20-120ft (6-37m)

Access: Boat

Expertise Rating: Intermediate

More likely than not you will see California's state fish, the garibaldi, at Bird Rock and throughout Southern California's waters. These protected damselfish are often curious about divers, making them ideal candidates for underwater portraits.

Catalina Marine Science Center Marine Life Refuge is a "no take, no-anchoring without permission" reserve that is about a half mile from Bird Rock. It extends for 1 mile, from Blue Cavern Point to the southwest end of Fisherman's Cove. Unlike most refuges, this one is posted with huge signs, legible from far offshore.

34 Isthmus Reef

Separated from Bird Rock by less than a quarter mile of open water, Isthmus Reef rises to within a few feet of the surface at low tide. A navigational hazard clearly marked by three buoys, Isthmus Reef has ripped the hulls out of many misdirected pleasure craft. Like Bird Rock, Isthmus Reef is about a quarter mile long and runs southeast to northwest.

Location: Front side of Catalina, Isthmus Harbor

Depth Range: 10-100ft (3-30m)

Access: Boat

Expertise Rating: Novice

A 10-minute boat ride from the Isthmus Harbor Landing, Isthmus Reef offers novice divers an ideal way to explore a scenic, shallow reef at their own pace. With excellent visibility, it's a good place to snorkel in the morning. In the afternoon the Isthmus wind and current can get pretty fierce.

The fairly steep, 30 to 40ft wall on the southwest face is riddled with cracks and chimneys. On the opening night of lobster season, this is a popular spot, because the chutes are usually crammed with bugs. Moray eels often share these quarters. Octopus dens are common near the bottom of the reef, which slopes gently to the sand at about 100ft. You can amuse yourself all day, however, without ever descending below 60ft.

BONNIE CARDONE

Garibaldi seem to flaunt their protected status.

35 Ship Rock

Ship Rock, a seamount that rises 66ft above the surface, shows sailors the way to Isthmus Harbor. On its north side, facing the channel, the pinnacle descends to the sandy seafloor at 120ft. To the south and west, shallow rocks and boilers make for tricky maneuvering and anchorage.

Depending on which way the current is running, you probably want to enter the water off the western or eastern side of the rock, descend quickly and ride the current along the deep, northern face of the reef while staying close to the bottom. This should give you plenty of time for sightseeing, a slow ascent and/or a safety stop and a 15-minute dive in the colorful, shallow kelp garden around the boilers.

Location: Front side of Catalina, outside Isthmus Harbor

Depth Range: 20-120ft (6-37m)

Access: Boat

Expertise Rating: Intermediate

The deep sand on the channel side is a well-known rest spot for angel sharks. In years past you might have seen 20 of them sleeping peacefully here. Possibly because they are easy marks for spearfishermen, angel sharks are not as common here as they once were.

Nevertheless, Ship Rock remains one of the most popular sites on Catalina because it is accessible, scenic, deep and relatively easy. Gorgonians wave in the current. Lobsters hide in the deep holes—at dawn and dusk you may find them scavenging on the sand.

Before returning to the boat, you may be able to salvage some expensive fishing gear or a small anchor from the area around the boilers on the eastern side of Ship Rock. This is a nice place to snorkel, but watch out for careless Jet Ski riders and boaters.

ANDREW SALLMON

Diver descends through schooling senorita wrasses.

36 Eagle Reef

Less than half a mile offshore, Eagle Reef is covered with dense kelp growth. If the kelp is lying flat beneath the surface, the channel current is running too hard for comfortable diving. If the kelp is standing straight or nearly straight, this is an excellent place to snorkel or scuba dive.

Perhaps a quarter mile long from east to west and 100 yards at its widest point, Eagle Reef is a pile of rocks and boulders, rising in stages from about 100ft to about 40ft. In some places the ledges are 20ft wide and the walls are 30ft high.

There are hundreds of lobsters on this reef, but they are pretty hard to find during the day because the structure is honeycombed with deep, narrow cracks and holes. They're easier to see at night, when your light accents their bright red shells. At night you will also find dozens of sheephead sleeping inside their mucous cocoons.

Large bait schools ride the channel current through here, attracting yellowtail, free-diving spearfishermen and sportfishing boats out of San Pedro. Dive charter boat captains take care to give fishing boats plenty of room, and so should you. These guys get mighty upset

Location: Front side of Catalina, about 1 mile (1.6km) W of Ship Rock, 1 mile (1.6km) E of Emerald Bay

Depth Range: 40-100ft (12-30m)

Access: Boat

Expertise Rating: Intermediate

if they think you're likely to tangle their lines or scare off the fish.

California spiny lobsters lack claws.

37 Cat Head Wall

Catalina ("Cat") Head towers several hundred feet above the western entrance to Catalina Harbor, the only safe haven for small craft on the weather side of the island. Beneath the surface, Cat Head Wall plunges almost vertically from just below the shoreline to well below the sport-diving limit.

It's a simple dive, but the best parts are deep. Descend along the wall as far as

Location: Back side of Catalina, W entrance to Catalina Harbor

Depth Range: 20-130ft (6-40m)

Access: Boat

Expertise Rating: Advanced

you'd like, monitor your computer, swim around a little, then ascend the wall. There's a lot of boat traffic and the isthmus tides can be quite strong, so dive up-current and try to navigate back to the boat beneath the surface. If you must surface before you reach the boat, do it as close to the wall as you can without getting caught in the surge.

Especially at depth, where horizontal visibility may extend to 50ft or more, there's a lot to see. You'll find large gorgonians, scallops, calico bass and sheephead clinging to or swimming around the clumps of rocks, gravelly rubble and boulders. Schools of barracuda, mackerel and yellowtail follow bait into Cat Harbor, so look up once in a while. At around 80ft you may find the debris of two shipwrecks.

Around the corner to the west, **Lobster Bay**, **Iron Bound Cove** and a string of nameless little inlets offer some shelter from the swell. If it's calm enough for a deep dive on Cat Head Wall, one of these inlets might make a nice, shallow second dive.

At Lobster Bay, patches of healthy kelp cling to the inshore reefs, formed mainly by rockslides. At 40 to 60ft the rocks tumble into the sand. In the past these rock piles provided habitat for large numbers of abalone and lobsters. In summer, giant sea bass—some as large as 500lbs—often cruise these walls.

A garibaldi swims from behind a golden gorgonian, as a stiff current flattens the kelp.

38 Farnsworth Bank

Location: Back side of Catalina, 5 miles (8km) S of Catalina Head

Depth Range: 60-130ft (18-40m)

Access: Boat

Expertise Rating: Advanced

One of Southern California's most popular and spectacular sites, Farnsworth Bank is a large seamount with several pinnacles and is more than half a mile wide from east to west. The two pinnacles at the western end are smaller than the main body of the seamount and isolated from it and each other by several hundred yards of very deep water. By itself, the larger seamount measures more than a quarter mile wide.

Because it's exposed to all weather, Farnsworth is most often visited in the calm, sunny days of high summer, when the water is usually very clear (100ft of vertical visibility is common) and, for this region, quite warm (70°F is about normal).

These conditions are wonderful for diving and for wide-angle photography, but they also make it easy to lose track of your depth and bottom time. No matter where you dive on Farnsworth, it gets very deep very quickly. Even in great weather, there may be a strong current. Buoyancy control and navigational skills are mandatory. It's an advanced site.

Invertebrate macrophotographic subjects thrive in the nutrient-rich currents: scallops, sea stars, nudibranchs, gorgeous fields of yellow and strawberry anemones, and purple hydrocoral (*Stylaster californicus*), to name a few. A slow-growing filter-feeding polyp, purple hydrocoral looks like its close relative, tropical staghorn coral. California hydrocorals, once collected as decorative objects, are now federally protected at Farnsworth.

Farnsworth Ecological Reserve includes the entire offshore seamount up to a depth of 250ft. In addition to California hydrocoral, no kelp, marine plants or geological specimens may be taken. Farnsworth Bank is also one of the last places where you may find white abalone *(Haliotis sorenseni),* a protected species now perhaps beyond the point of no return. In hopes of reviving the white abalone, the National Marine Fisheries Service has undertaken a project to collect healthy adults of both sexes. If you see one, don't touch it. Make a careful note of its location and inform the boat captain.

Large pelagics such as barracuda, yellowtail, white sea bass and blue sharks frequent Farnsworth. You may also see resident sheephead, blacksmiths, calico bass and electric rays.

ANDREW SALLMON
Purple hydrocoral and a red gorgonian share a rocky reef.

San Clemente Island Dive Sites

San Clemente Island lies about 20 miles due south of Santa Catalina, across the Outer Santa Barbara Passage. It's a two- or three-hour run from either Avalon or Catalina Harbor to most of the dive sites on the front side of San Clemente, four or five hours from San Pedro or Long Beach, and a little longer from San Diego. The island runs northwest to southeast, almost parallel to Catalina.

Although San Clemente is no farther west than Catalina, the mainland coast cuts southeast along Orange and northern San Diego Counties, so San Clemente is quite a bit farther offshore. It's a longer boat ride, and the weather is often quite a bit rougher.

The U.S. Navy uses San Clemente as an artillery-bombing range, and there is a S.E.A.L. facility in Northwest Harbor. When the Navy holds live-fire exercises, it closes all or part of the area to civilian boat traffic. For years, environmentalists concerned with the effect on marine life have tried to persuade the Navy to stop bombing the island.

Live Ammunition

If you swim over something that looks like a bomb or an artillery shell, assume it is live, no matter how thoroughly encrusted. Do not bring it back to the boat for all to admire. Get away from it and report its location to the captain.

Not surprisingly, dive boats visit San Clemente much less frequently than they visit Catalina. That's a shame, because in good weather the reefs and coves around San Clemente are as beautiful as any in Southern California. Like Catalina, the sheltered front side of San Clemente is often calm. At Fish Hook Cove, Little Flower and Windowpane, vertical visibility often approaches 100ft.

San Clemente Island Dive Sites	Good Snorkeling	Novice	Intermediate	Advanced
39 Nine Fathom Reef				●
40 Seal Cove Caverns				●
41 Sun Point				●
42 Fish Hook Cove	●	●		●
43 Little Flower	●			●
44 Windowpane				●

San Clemente is known for large game fish, especially yellowtail and white sea bass, in the blue water outside the reefs around China Point, Pyramid Cove and Pyramid Head. Some of the biggest calico bass in Southern California live in the dense kelp inside China Point and Pyramid Cove.

Pink and green abalone have suffered from disease and overharvesting, but some remain on the back side, on the beautiful but rarely visited shallow reefs near Mail Point and Lost Point. All around the island, colorful gorgonians, nudibranchs and anemones flourish, creating excellent macrophotographic opportunities at almost any depth. Nine Fathom Reef, often a drift dive because of the strong current, has a spectacular invertebrate forest of purple hydrocorals and gorgonians.

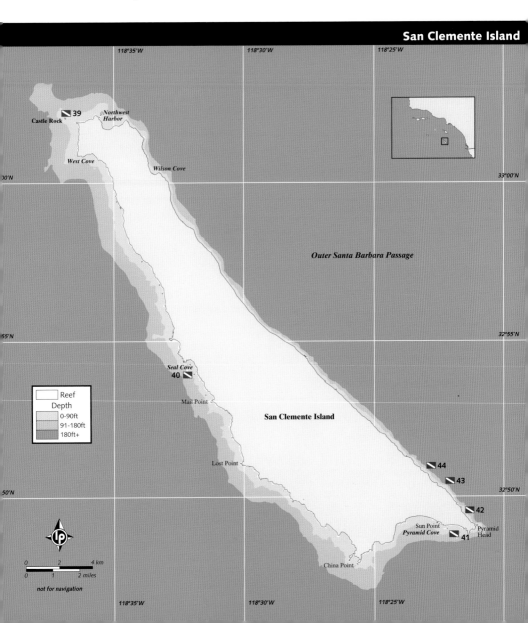

39 Nine Fathom Reef

Nine Fathom Reef is a medium-depth, world-class dive off the northwest face of San Clemente Island. Because the current is usually quite strong, this is an advanced site. If the weather is good, some boat captains will allow experienced divers to do this as a drift dive.

North of the reef, the bottom falls away into the deep water of the Santa

Location: NW face of San Clemente, N of Castle Rock

Depth Range: 60-90ft (18-27m)

Access: Boat

Expertise Rating: Advanced

ANDREW SALLMON

Red gorgonians add a splash of color to Nine Fathom Reef.

Barbara Passage. South of the reef, toward the island, is a large shoal. Large boats cannot navigate safely in this area. If divers allow the current to sweep them into it, they may have a problem getting back to the boat.

Nine Fathom Reef has much in common with **Farnsworth Bank** (a few miles due north, off the back side of Catalina). Nine Fathom usually has exceptionally clear, warm water. It's a great place to see large pelagics, such as yellowtail, white sea bass, mola-mola and black sea bass.

It is also one of the few sites where you can find purple hydrocoral (*Stylaster californicus*). Unlike Farnsworth, however, Nine Fathom Reef (which is dived a lot less often) has abundant, intact hydrocorals as shallow as

65ft. In high summer, when water temperatures sometimes approach 75°F, drifting over Nine Fathom Reef's hydrocoral growths is about as close as you can get to tropical diving in Southern California.

BONNIE CARDONE

Slow-growing hydrocoral rarely exceeds 2ft (.6m) in diameter.

40 Seal Cove Caverns

A short distance southeast of Seal Cove (around the midpoint of San Clemente's seaward side), below a dense kelp stand in about 50ft of water, there is a smallish network of submarine caves. None of them exceed 50ft from end to end, so it is always possible to see the proverbial light at the end of the tunnel. They are also roomy enough to penetrate without risk of getting stuck.

Since it's relatively shallow and exposed to the weather, Seal Cove Caverns is usually fairly murky. On a good day you might get as much as 40ft of horizontal visibility, but you don't need to see very far inside a cave, so it really doesn't matter.

Location: Back side of San Clemente, about 7 miles (11km) NW of China Pt.

Depth Range: 40-50ft (12-15m)

Access: Boat

Expertise Rating: Advanced

Calico bass, sheephead and rockfish take shelter in these caves. Sea fans, scallops and anemones cling to the walls and ceilings. Mobs of young lobsters cluster in the antechambers. But the thing about cave diving is, you never know what you might find.

41 Sun Point

From China Point to Pyramid Cove, dense kelp covers the inshore reefs of San Clemente Island's south face, providing habitat for lobsters, calico bass, cabezon and sheephead. The dramatic sites known as **Boiler Wall** and **Inside Boilers** are between Sun Point and Pyramid Head.

Location: Back side of San Clemente, S face of Pyramid Head, near Sun Pt.

Depth Range: 30-130ft (9.1-40m)

Access: Boat

Expertise Rating: Advanced

The top of Boiler Wall, about 100 yards south of the boiler rocks, lies below thick kelp in about 40ft. A complex structure with pinnacles, sand channels, ledges and sheer walls, Boiler Wall descends steeply toward the open sea, eventually reaching depths below 130ft.

The water is often quite calm and clear, providing excellent opportunities for wide-angle photography. Macrophotographers will enjoy the fields of gorgonians, nudibranchs and anemones.

Inside Boilers rises from about 60ft to just a few feet below the surface. Boats usually anchor near the spacious main entrance to an extensive network of caverns.

In addition to the house-sized front door, you can safely enter and exit through any of several large chimneys. These also serve to light the large, colorful gorgonians hanging from the ceilings and walls. On a warm, calm, sunny day, with 100ft of visibility and water temperatures in the low 70s, these caves are reminiscent of the tropics.

42 Fish Hook Cove

Protected by the inward-curving rocky outcropping that gives this site its name, Fish Hook Cove is really two sites. The sheltered area, characterized by calm, shallow water, scattered rocks and kelp, eelgrass, white sand and small reef fish, is ideal for novice scuba divers and snorkelers.

Location: Front side of San Clemente, about 1 mile (1.6km) from SE end

Depth Range:
20-60ft (6-18m) (inside cove)
60-130ft+ (18-40m+) (outside cove)

Access: Boat

Expertise Rating: Novice (inside cove)
Advanced (outside cove)

Advanced divers will enjoy the area outside the cove, near the end of the hook-shaped reef, where the bottom drops away with astonishing abruptness. This wall is known for its abundant moray eels.

The outside wall is very popular with blue-water hunters. Less than 100 yards offshore you'll find brilliantly clear water 250ft deep. Because of the steep drop-off and the presence of large schools of bait, the wall is a natural "run" for schools of hungry pelagics like yellowtail, mackerel and barracuda.

Deep, clear inshore water is common along San Clemente's southeast end, but free-divers should watch for severe surface currents, which are common there.

The calm, shallow waters of Fish Hook Cove are great for novice divers and snorkelers.

43 Little Flower

Like Fish Hook, Little Flower has a steep, deep outside northern wall and a shallower, sheltered, less precipitous southern slope. This underwater islet rises from the depths to within 30ft of the surface. It looks roughly like a flower on the NOAA chart, hence the name.

In summer Little Flower is famous for the huge schools of bonita, barracuda, mackerel and especially yellowtail that frequent the area. When the baitfish begin to form tight, shimmering balls, look for these magnificent predators to come streaking in from deep water. Feeding yellowtail seem compelled to investigate everything they see. In an instant you may find yourself completely encircled by a whirling, shiny mass of silver and yellow.

Location: Front side of San Clemente, about a mile (1.6km) NW of Fishhook Cove

Depth Range: 30-130ft (9.1-40m)

Access: Boat

Expertise Rating: Advanced

Near the shallower rocks you'll find calico bass (some in the 8 to 10lb range), moray eels and the usual assortment of photogenic small reef fish and invertebrates. On the southern slope there is usually not a lot of current, especially at scuba diving depths. But in the open water at the surface, it can be like diving in a river.

44 Windowpane

This inshore seamount may be the most intensely beautiful dive on San Clemente Island. The water is usually so clear that you hardly need a dive light to see the true colors of the anemones and gorgonians that cover the structure, or to see the moray eels that inhabit almost every hole.

Windowpane is so beautiful and so deceptively close to shore that divers may underestimate its challenges—with disastrous results. The water may be clear and warm, but this is a deep dive, often with a strong current. Dive conservatively—the nearest hyperbaric chamber is at the Isthmus on Catalina.

Boats anchor on one of two adjacent pinnacles, or in the saddle between. South

Location: Front side of San Clemente, about 3 miles (4.8km) NW of SE end

Depth Range: 60-130ft (18-40m)

Access: Boat

Expertise Rating: Advanced

of the seamount, the bottom falls away quickly—within 200 yards it's 200ft deep. Though a surface current is common, it may slacken considerably below 30ft. If the boat has a bow gate, exit there and follow the anchor line to the pinnacle.

Not all boats have a bow gate. What then? If the surface current is running hard, take a compass bearing on the anchor line before you jump. Descend as soon as you hit the water, get under the current, swim to the bow and follow the anchor line to the seamount.

If you can't get under the current, abort the dive. Swim across the current, grab the current line and pull yourself in. Do not attempt to swim at the surface against a strong current. You risk hyperventilation and exhaustion. If you are swept into the deep water behind the boat, do not descend. With no visual references, you risk an uncontrolled descent.

The water may be calm at depth, but don't forget the current above. Dive up-current of the anchor. Most of the best stuff—invertebrates, morays, reef fish and stunning vistas—is below 90ft. Return to the anchor and use it as your ascent line. Save enough air for a safety stop.

ANDREW SALLMON

Windowpane offers stunning wide-angle vistas.

Santa Barbara Island Dive Sites

The smallest of the South Channel Islands, and the only one within the boundaries of Channel Islands National Park, Santa Barbara lies more than 40 miles (64km) west of San Pedro, 40 miles (64km) south of Ventura, and 20 miles (32km) west of Catalina's west end. Within the Ecological Reserve, which covers the entire front (eastern) side from South Point to Arch Point, no invertebrates may be taken in less than 20ft (6m) of water. For Santa Barbara's once-flourishing abalone population, this regulation is too little and too late.

Point Conception and the North Channel Islands offer some protection from the northwest swell, but Santa Barbara is open to weather from the south and west. The front side is fairly sheltered except in heavy weather, but the most exciting sites are on the weather sides, to the north and west of the island

The island is a seamount, perhaps a square mile of which breaks the surface. It is almost entirely ringed by rocky shoals. Inshore navigation, especially at night, can be tricky. On the front side there's a huge sea lion rookery. For some this is Santa Barbara's greatest attraction. Near the midpoint of the north side, elephant seals have established a colony.

Open to the strong ocean currents, Santa Barbara is a great fish trap. Yellowtail, white sea bass, barracuda, and even migratory pelagics like tuna, marlin and

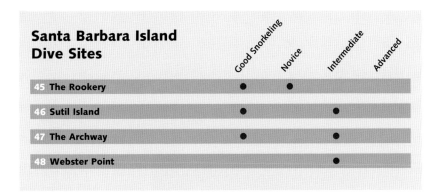

Santa Barbara Island Dive Sites	Good Snorkeling	Novice	Intermediate	Advanced
45 The Rookery	●	●		
46 Sutil Island	●		●	
47 The Archway	●		●	
48 Webster Point			●	

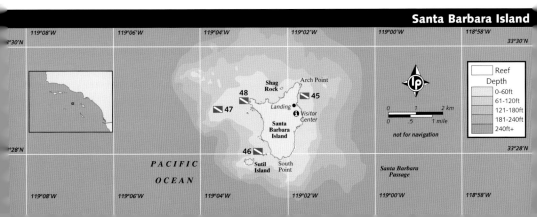

Santa Barbara Island

swordfish visit these waters to feed on sardines and smelt. Blue-water hunters say Santa Barbara compares well with San Clemente Island as a spearfishing site. The docile, giant sea bass is also known to frequent Santa Barbara's outer walls.

The water is usually warmer than it is in the North Channel, about the same as Catalina's back side. In the narrow channel between Sutil Island and Santa Barbara Island, the current keeps the water pretty clean, and the visibility can be spectacular.

Where there are game fish and marine mammals, there are sharks: blues and makos, even the occasional great white. A few years ago, in what may have been a mighty territorial display, a great white repeatedly rammed a dive boat in front of the rookery.

45 The Rookery

You can hear the sea lion rookery as you approach Santa Barbara Island, even when you are still miles away. In early summer, when they give birth and mate, thousands of raucous, squabbling sea lions cover most of the steep, 250ft hillside.

The strongest males attract a harem of females that they will defend against all competitors. The half-ton bulls fatten up all year for the chance to mate, which occurs immediately after the cows give birth to the previous season's offspring. In the crowded rookery, pups sometimes perish, accidentally trampled in a skir-

Location: Front side of Santa Barbara, between the Landing and Arch Pt.

Depth Range: 20-40ft (6-12m)

Access: Boat

Expertise Rating: Novice

mish or deliberately killed by frustrated losers.

During the rut (in early summer), even young animals may bare their teeth, blow bubbles at you or nip at your fins in aggressive display. Usually it's a bluff, but a 40lb yearling is strong enough to knock you on your wallet. Always treat sea lions with caution and respect. Allow them to initiate any interaction. If they don't seem to want to interact with you, leave them alone.

You can recognize an adult male by his size and his dome-shaped forehead. If a bull approaches you in

BONNIE CARDONE
Sea lions cover the steep southern slope of Santa Barbara Island.

the water, back off. He may see you as a potential rival. After the bulls head north in July, the rookery calms down considerably. The nursing females remain until September, when they wean most of the pups. Sub-adults of both sexes live on the island year-round.

Inshore, the pups learn to swim in nursery pools. Stay out of these. Females have nasty canines and are protective of their young. Moreover, you could be cited and fined for violating the Marine Mammal Protection Act. There is a national park ranger station on the island.

Most times of the year, the younger sea lions on Santa Barbara seem to delight in the company of divers. Usually this is the last dive site of the day. As soon you drop anchor, a mob of sub-adult sea lions races toward the boat, barking ecstatical-

ly. They'll entertain you endlessly as you sit on the sand or swim with them in about 30ft of water.

Their play is graceful and creative, evocative and communicative. A young female who bellies down on the sand and looks over her shoulder may be flirting, but don't take it personally. Sub-adults engage in frequent mock copulation.

If you try to copy their maneuvers, they may imitate, improvise upon or possibly make fun of your efforts. It's even more fun to snorkel with them, because you're less encumbered and better able to keep up. As long as you take care to stay outside the nursery, you can ride the surf with them toward the beach. You can never tell what an animal is feeling, but they seem to enjoy these moments as much as we do.

46 Sutil Island

Sutil Island is a pinnacle of the Santa Barbara Island seamount formation, separated from the main island by a narrow saddleback channel that is a few hundred yards wide and no deeper than 60ft. In midchannel, several rocks break the surface and many others rise to within 20ft of it. There is thick kelp all around Sutil and along the southwest face of Santa Barbara Island.

Due to the strong channel current, the water is usually exceptionally clean, so it's a favorite site for snorkelers and spearfishermen. If the baitfish are there, big schools of yellowtail come charging through in the morning and late afternoon. White sea bass, which feed mostly at night on squid, sleep during the day in the inshore

Location: About ¼ mile (.4km) off the SW corner of Santa Barbara

Depth Range: 20-130ft (6-40m)

Access: Boat

Expertise Rating: Intermediate

BONNIE CARDONE

Divers prepare to descend into Sutil's kelp forest.

kelp beds, where the current is usually comparatively light.

The rocky structures that surround Sutil Island are shallow—60ft or so—for about 200 yards to seaward. Farther out the topography becomes more dramatic, with canyons, caves and steep walls that drop for 50ft.

West of Sutil, the bottom drops away to more than 120ft, but it's not necessary to make a deep dive to enjoy these reefs. In the 60 to 90ft range, scuba divers will encounter reef fish, pinnipeds and lobsters. Gorgonians, scallops and nudibranchs provide opportunities for macrophotography.

Sutil Island is riddled with sea caves. The deeper caves are often chock-full of lobsters, while the caves above the water-line are used as haul-outs by harbor seals and sea lions. Due to the current and surge, it is often unsafe to enter the underwater caves without proper training and equipment.

47 The Archway

More than half a mile offshore, the rocky formation called **Seven Fathom Reef** lies on the western edge of a wide shoal. Its most striking feature is a large natural archway, more than 20ft wide and 30ft tall, the top of which creates boilers where it nearly breaks the surface.

Location: About ⅔ mile (1km) W of Webster Pt., Santa Barbara

Depth Range: 30-100ft (9.1-30m)

Access: Boat

Expertise Rating: Intermediate

Scuba divers love to explore this beautiful structure, overgrown with anemones, sponges and gorgonians. Large scallops occupy the lower regions, and lobsters hide in the cracks and holes.

If you follow the south face of the reef toward the island, you'll find a large cave about 100ft below the surface. Lobsters often shelter in the upper, nether reaches of this cave. Take a compass reading before you enter. If you disturb the loose silt on the bottom, you can quickly blot out all light and lose your bearings.

West of the reef you're quickly in more than 150ft of water. Where the cold, nutritious water of the depths rises to meet the warm water of the shoal, baitfish come to feed on the plentiful plankton.

ANDREW SALLMON

A photographer examines the Archway's rubble.

The baitfish attract schools of barracuda and yellowtail, and in high summer great game fish such as tuna and marlin often swim through the area. Blue-water hunters love this spot, as well as a similar structure called **Hidden Reef**, about a half mile north-northwest of The Archway.

48 Webster Point

Webster Point is a small headland that projects northwest off the main body of Santa Barbara Island. Inshore navigation around the promontory is treacherous, as it is ringed with rocks and boilers. On its western face you'll find safe anchorage atop a reef system marked by kelp stands.

At 30 to 40ft the reeftop's surface is unremarkable, but as you descend its outer walls, you'll enter an extremely complex maze of tunnels, caves, chimneys and walls. All kinds of critters find shelter within this submarine housing project: reef fish, nudibranchs, octopuses. Bat rays often lie in the sand channels between the fingers of the reef. Curious sea lions may swim by to check you out.

At 90ft, beneath a ledge on the southeast side of Webster Point, is the

Location: NW corner of Santa Barbara

Depth Range: 40-90ft (12-27m)

Access: Boat

Expertise Rating: Intermediate

entrance to **Dragon Cave**. Deep within, a hole in the reef lets in shafts of light from above. At some points in the cave you can't see the entrance, but there is little danger of getting lost or stuck. Just follow the chamber until it exits on the shallow side of the reef. It is a fairly deep dive, however, and an entrancing one, so keep an eye on your computer and your air supply.

ANDREW SALLMON

California sea lions are often curious about divers.

San Nicolas Island Dive Sites

Sixty miles offshore, San Nicolas Island is actually a little closer to Ventura Harbor than it is to San Pedro and Long Beach. From any of these it's often a rather bumpy six- or seven-hour voyage. Boats bound for San Nicolas may end up elsewhere due to bad weather.

There's a large naval base on the island. The Navy grants access to civilian vessels on a per-trip basis, but it can revoke permission with little or no warning. So, you may set out for San Nick at midnight, only to find yourself at Santa Rosa or Santa Barbara in the morning, even in good weather.

Only 7 miles long by 3 miles wide, Nick is not very popular with underwater photographers and sightseers. Wind and swell continually buffet the island, so the water tends to be a lot murkier and a few degrees colder than at Catalina, San Clemente or Anacapa. In heavy north-swell conditions, boats may be forced to anchor at Dutch Harbor and dive on the rather uninteresting south side of the island.

As is the case with Santa Rosa in the North Channel, many divers come to San Nicolas to take game. Halibut hunters love San Nicolas' extensive areas of sandy bottom, and lobster grabbers have taken some humongous bugs from the rocky sites known as The Boilers, The Freeway and Alpha Breakers. Elephant seals and sea lions have colonized several beaches on the west end.

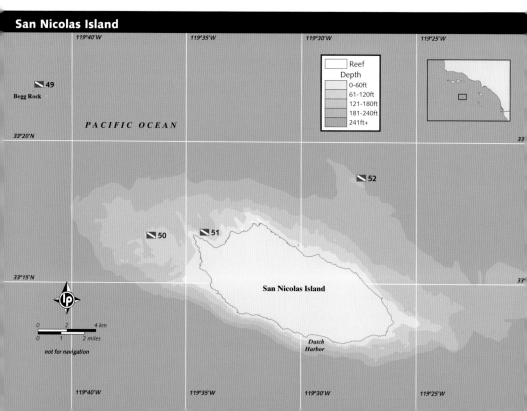

In calm weather the scattered kelp stands in the coves and around the reefs can be quite scenic, but for sightseers and photographers, Begg Rock is Nick's big draw. Arguably the most beautiful seamount in Southern California, Begg Rock attracts divers from all around the world. Boats that intend to visit Begg list it as their principal destination.

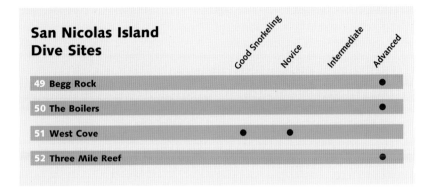

San Nicolas Island Dive Sites	Good Snorkeling	Novice	Intermediate	Advanced
49 Begg Rock				●
50 The Boilers				●
51 West Cove	●	●		
52 Three Mile Reef				●

49 Begg Rock

Begg Rock is a spectacular system of reefs and pinnacles, some of which plunge vertically to depths of more than 200ft. Plumose anemones, strawberry anemones, giant scallops, sponges of every color, sea stars and cowries cling to every square inch of surface area. In the midst of this chaos, beautifully camouflaged sculpin and octopuses hide in plain view. Vermilion rockfish school placidly in the deep hollows.

Begg Rock rises a few feet above the surface at the north end of the western reef. Two steep, inner walls, one running north-south, the other east-west, form a right angle at a depth of about 80ft, perhaps 50 yards south of the wash rocks.

Unprotected from wind and swell, this site is seldom visited in winter. In mild summer weather the sheltered area between the inside walls is usually calm and clear. In this vast amphitheater, visibility sometimes exceeds 100ft, affording

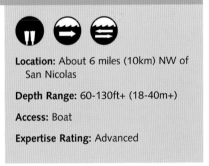

Location: About 6 miles (10km) NW of San Nicolas

Depth Range: 60-130ft+ (18-40m+)

Access: Boat

Expertise Rating: Advanced

BONNIE CARDONE

Sessile marine life clings to Begg Rock's surface.

divers an amazing view of the seamount rising from the sand.

Depending on conditions, boats anchor outside the reef (to the west) or on a third seamount less than 100 yards east of the wash rocks. If you're anchored east of the rocks, the deep corner is a few yards south. If you're outside, anchored on either of the main walls, just follow the anchor line over the reef to the inside

face. In the shallower areas on top of the reef, the surge can be quite powerful.

In good weather most boats allow two dives here. Although navigation is simple, there is a significant risk of exceeding safe depth and time limits, especially if you make more than one dive. One ought to make a few supervised deep dives in cold water with poor surface visibility before attempting Begg Rock.

50 The Boilers

Not far off the west end of San Nicolas Island is a wide shoal called The Boilers. Directly to the east is a barren, open area known as **The Freeway**. Depending on where you anchor, you can dive in depths from 20 to 80ft. Above 30ft the surge is usually very powerful.

At almost any depth, visibility typically doesn't exceed 20ft. Strong currents are also characteristic of these sites. To dive here, you must navigate well with a compass and be comfortable in rough water.

You'll find a few interesting short walls and ledges, as well as some kelp growth, on The Boilers and bordering The Freeway, but neither site is particularly scenic.

Location: About 1½ miles (2.4km) W of San Nicolas

Depth Range: 20-80ft (6-24m)

Access: Boat

Expertise Rating: Advanced

Rockfish, sheephead, calico bass, lingcod and ocean whitefish are common. You can find scallops, nudibranchs and other invertebrates on the rocks, but it's hard to stay in one place long enough to take pictures.

Nonetheless, if you visit San Nick in the fall or winter, you will likely dive either or both of these sites. Moreover, the divers on-board will probably fall all over one another in their eagerness. Why? To hunt for lobsters, which are big and plentiful. If you hit the right narrow ledge or shallow hole, you can bag your limit in one dive.

ANDREW SALLMON

The territorial China rockfish is an excellent model.

Bug Grabbing

From mid-September to mid-March, any diver with a current California fishing license and an Ocean Enhancement Stamp may take the tasty California spiny lobster (*Panulirus interruptus*). While big ones are no longer common, "bugs" remain abundant.

The daily bag limit is seven. On a two-day charter you may possess 14 at the end of the trip. You can't use anything except your hands to catch them, and you must carry a lobster gauge (approved by the Department of Fish and Game) while in the water. You may bring a lobster to the surface, but not aboard a vessel or ashore, for purposes of measuring.

The minimum size limit is 3¼ inches (8.25mm), measured along the back of the body shell. To measure a bug, place one end of the gauge midway between its eyes, snug against the front edge of the shell. If the other end of the gauge falls on the body shell, the bug is legal. If the span of the gauge exceeds the span of the shell, release it. If pinnipeds are in the area, conscientious divers return "short" bugs to the safety of the reef. Many divers also release egg-bearing females, no matter how large (the eggs, borne on the abdomen, look a bit like caviar).

Lobster hunting requires skill, strength and concentration. Bugs are wary critters. During the day they rarely come out of their holes. To find them, swim slowly over the reef or rock pile scanning for a glimpse of antennae or crawl through the eelgrass till you find a small ledge, then follow it. When they've molted, lobsters feel safest in the eelgrass.

Lobsters are nocturnal scavengers, so the season's opening night is a big event. Hundreds of divers hit the water just before midnight, hoping to catch unwary bugs in the open. At night the red shell shows clearly in the beam of your dive light, even if the bug is in a hole. Most bug divers carry small pocket lights during the day.

Get as close as you can without spooking it (a fine art), then grab as fast as you can. Aim behind it—lobsters propel themselves backward to escape. If you get a hand on one, it'll cling to the rock with its powerful legs. Get a grip on its body, then shake and pull until it lets go. (Antennae may break off—if your quarry escapes, it will grow new ones after the next molt.) Holding on firmly, open your bag with your free hand and stuff the lobster in, tail first. Leave your lobster intact in the bag until you reach the dock. (They can live a long time out of water.) A game warden may fine you if your bug can't be measured.

Lobsters leave the reef's recesses to scavenge at night.

51 West Cove

A sheltered area at the west end of San Nicolas, West Cove is one of the few spots on the island that's often calm enough for novice divers, snorkelers and photographers. It's usually the last dive of the day and is about as scenic a dive as you'll find on San Nick.

At the cove's entrance, there is an intricate network of relatively shallow, kelpy reefs, inhabited by small reef fish and invertebrates: calico bass, senorita

Location: NW side of San Nicolas

Depth Range: 20-60ft (6-18m)

Access: Boat

Expertise Rating: Novice

wrasses, sheephead, surfperch, nudibranchs, cowries and anemones.

Between the reefs, as well as inshore, there are wide expanses of fine white sand. In summer, halibut spawn in West Cove (as well as all around the island's topographically unremarkable eastern half).

At West Cove, divers routinely encounter sea lions from the nearby rookery. Just around the corner, elephant seals come ashore to mate, give birth and molt. Mainly in fall and winter, you'll see them on the beach.

BONNIE CARDONE

Fish flit amid West Cove's shallow, kelpy reefs.

52 Three Mile Reef

When the Navy denies access to San Nick's inshore reefs, and the weather out of the north is mild, Three Mile Reef is an excellent alternative site. This seamount runs for about half a mile east to west, is surrounded by 200ft of water and rises to about 70ft below the surface.

Location: Front side of San Nicolas

Depth Range: 80-120ft (24-37m)

Access: Boat

Expertise Rating: Advanced

Like most offshore seamounts, it's a challenging and exciting dive, requiring strong navigational skills and the ability to handle current and poor surface visibility.

Visited less often than many other sites, Three Mile Reef remains fairly pristine. Beneath the plankton bloom, the water is often clear and calm. Invertebrate macro-photographic subjects are abundant: scallops, nudibranchs, sponges, tunicates, anemones and giant keyhole limpets. You'll find rockfish and lingcod amid the deeper rocks, ocean whitefish and sheephead nearer the surface, and lobsters hiding in the cracks and holes.

BONNIE CARDONE

Giant keyhole limpets, California's largest limpet, can grow to 5 inches (13cm) long.

The Banks Dive Sites

About 100 miles from the mainland, Cortes Bank is a huge seamount, larger overall than Catalina Island, most of it too deep for scuba diving. Tanner Bank, a similar structure about half the size of Cortes, lies 20 miles to the north. Boats that visit Cortes often stop to dive at Tanner on the way out.

These distant, offshore banks are rarely visited by divers. Most of those who come are blue-water hunters (during the summer) and lobster grabbers (in October). During the winter and spring it's usually just too rough to dive here. Even on the best days the current can be fearsome. Often, a dense fog steams off the surface. A hundred miles from shore, these are risky conditions.

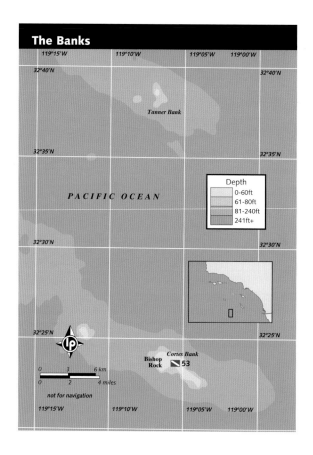

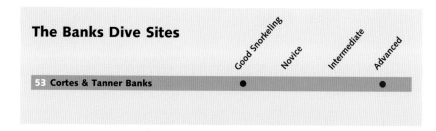

Safe Diving on Deep Reefs & Seamounts

Begg Rock, Richardson Rock, Farnsworth Bank and the other deep reefs and seamounts of Southern California are among the most beautiful dive sites in the world, but they are more demanding than deep dives in the tropics.

Most deep (90ft or 30m) boat dives in Southern California are advanced sites, often complicated by current and poor water clarity near the surface. Southern California dive boats rarely provide in-water divemasters or tour guides. However, most dive shops offer several deep-diving classes per year. One ought to make several supervised deep dives wearing a full wetsuit and weight belt before attempting these sites.

The divemaster will probably stress the importance of following the anchor line all the way to the reef. If there's a current running when a boat drops anchor on a deep reef or seamount, it will play out a lot of anchor line. Directly beneath the boat, the water may be much deeper than the top of the reef. If you stray from the anchor line, you may miss the reef and descend far beyond the depths of safe recreational diving.

It is possible to make two or three deep boat dives in one day, but avoid pushing your limits for depth and bottom time, especially with repetitive dives. Monitor your computer and gauges at regular intervals, maybe once a minute. You don't have a lot of time or air. Don't become so engrossed that you forget where you are. At 120ft (36m), you will require two minutes to make a safe ascent, without a safety stop.

It is advisable to incorporate a pony bottle or a Spare Air in your gear, for emergencies only. If something goes wrong at extreme depth, a buddy may not respond quickly enough to help. Think in terms of self-sufficiency.

Unless an emergency prevents it, always begin your ascent from a deep dive with enough air for a controlled ascent and a safety decompression stop. Navigate back to the anchor or the ascent line, monitor the computer while ascending, then hang off for at least five minutes at 15ft (5m). Properly weighted (neutral at 15ft or 5m after you've nearly emptied your tank), you should be able to make a safe, controlled, free ascent, even if you can't find the ascent line or anchor chain.

DAVID MCCRAY

53 Cortes & Tanner Banks

A bell buoy marks the boiler rocks at the highest spot on Cortes Bank. Around the buoy, perhaps 10 sq miles of Cortes is shallow enough to dive—parts of it rise to within a few feet of the surface. Near the buoy lies the wreck of the *Jalisco*, which sank more than 30 years ago. It is possible to explore the wreck under calm conditions, but due to constant surge, penetration is unsafe. A few miles west, another pinnacle rises to 54ft.

Tanner Bank, which lies 20 miles north, also reaches as high as 54ft, but the diveable area at Tanner is smaller than the diveable area at Cortes.

The banks are the only shallow structures for many miles in every direction. Consequently, their crystal-clear waters are full of baitfish and game fish, riding the current. When the water gets warm, the big fish come from the south: tuna, dorado, marlin, yellowtail and sharks.

Location: About 100 miles (160km) S of Ventura, 100 miles (160km) W of San Diego

Depth Range: 80-130ft (24-40m)

Access: Boat

Expertise Rating: Advanced

The banks are one of Southern California's most advanced sites, and for experienced divers they are also among the most exciting. Sheephead and calico bass inhabit the shallower reefs, and purple hydrocoral is found at most depths. Scorpionfish rest on the bottom, while barracuda and baitfish spiral in midwater. In September migrating lobsters march single file across the sand. In summer, game fish chase sardine schools, and blue sharks clean up the scraps.

DAVID MCCRAY

The California scorpionfish's cryptic markings and coloration help it blend in with its surroundings.

San Diego Dive Sites

San Diego's Mission Bay is the jumping-off point to four major dive areas: Wreck Alley, Point Loma, Point La Jolla and the Coronado Islands. With the exception of the Coronados, all of these are close to the mainland, subject to swell, boat traffic and pollution—conditions that typically make mainland diving somewhat less attractive than diving at the Channel Islands. Nevertheless, each of these areas has merits of its own, whether it is easy accessibility or diveable wrecks.

Wreck Alley is probably the best-known site, drawing divers from every part of the world. New Hope Rock (an inshore kelp dive off Point Loma) and Wreck Alley are often packaged together as a half-day boat trip from Mission Bay.

Many of the sites around Point La Jolla are shore dives, discussed in the South Channel Shore Dive Sites section. The Coronado Islands, which San Diego boats visit regularly, lie a few miles south of the Mexican border. For information about them see the Lonely Planet Pisces Books' *Diving & Snorkeling Baja California*.

San Diego

117°20'W | 117°15'W

Point La Jolla

La Jolla

Gulf Of Santa Catalina

32°50'N

32°50'N

Depth
- 0-60ft
- 61-120ft
- 121ft+

Pacific Beach

Mission Bay

Mission Beach

54

Ocean Beach

32°45'N | 32°45'N

0   2   4 km
0   1   2 miles

not for navigation

209   San Diego Bay

Coronado Island

55

Point Loma

117°20'W | 117°15'W

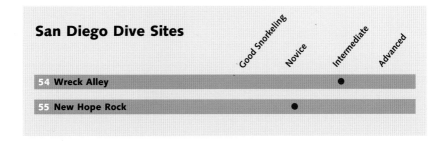

San Diego Dive Sites	Good Snorkeling	Novice	Intermediate	Advanced
54 Wreck Alley			●	
55 New Hope Rock		●		

54   Wreck Alley

In 1986 three vessels were scuttled off the coast of San Diego to benefit divers and to serve as artificial reefs. Known as Wreck Alley, this area has become one of the most popular San Diego dive destinations. Over the years, several more wrecks have joined the sunken fleet's ranks.

Though not a particularly deep dive, it can be dangerous—injuries and fatalities have occurred. Listen carefully to your pre-dive briefing and dive conservatively. Wreck Alley is not an ideal site for your first Southern California dive, especially if you have not yet mastered buoyancy control with a 7mm full wetsuit and weights.

The **HMCS Yukon** is the newest and by far the most popular of the wrecks. On the night of July 14, 2000, a day ahead of schedule, the 360ft Canadian destroyer became the centerpiece of San Diego's Wreck Alley.

Location: About ¼ mile (.4km) off Mission Beach, San Diego

Depth Range: 60-90ft (18-27m)

Access: Boat

Expertise Rating: Intermediate

The *Yukon* was towed into position above her final resting place on July 12. Though scheduled to be scuttled at 9am on July 15, the ship began to flood around 11pm on July 14, possibly due to the hundred holes that were cut in the *Yukon* to allow for diver penetration. The crew abandoned ship without detonating the explosives with which they had planned to scuttle her.

Now cleared of explosives, the *Yukon* lies on her side in 100ft of water (not on her keel as was planned) just north of the *Ruby E*, a 165ft U.S. Coast Guard Cutter, scuttled in 1987. Eventually the *Yukon* will become a living reef, covered with scallops, gorgonians and anemones, as is the *Ruby E* today. The tops of both wrecks reach to about 55 or 60ft. The *Ruby E* rests on a 90ft bottom.

Water clarity is typical for inshore Southern California, from 10 to 40ft, not always good enough for wide-angle photography, but more

ANDREW SALLMON
Though visibility is often limited, the *Yukon* offers many features that warrant a closer look.

than adequate for macrophotography. In addition to invertebrates like lobsters and octopuses, you'll find lots of small reef fish on the *Ruby E* (and soon enough on the *Yukon*): calico bass, garibaldi, senorita wrasses and the like.

Wreck Alley is a 20-minute boat ride from Mission Bay. Some Mission Bay dive-charter operators allow penetration of some wrecks, including the *Yukon*. Some offer wreck-diving certification classes. Be sure to ask what your options are before booking. For more information see the Listings section.

ANDREW SALLMON

Eventually the *Yukon* will be a living reef.

55 New Hope Rock

A scenic kelp dive, New Hope Rock is often the second stop (after Wreck Alley) for half-day boat trips out of Mission Bay. Part of Point Loma's mile-long string of rocky high spots in about 50ft of water, New Hope Rock creates a boiler area about a quarter mile off the beach, just north of the point.

In the past, dive charters tended to favor the Point La Jolla reef, a few miles north of Wreck Alley, but much of the kelp forest has died off there in recent years. Point Loma, to the south, is closer to port, and the kelp there remains relatively healthy.

New Hope Rock provides habitat for lobsters, scallops, octopuses, nudibranchs, anemones, garibaldi and sheephead. All around the reef, calico bass and olive rockfish hide in the dense kelp. It's a pleasant dive and a good place for novices (or divers new to Southern California) to get accustomed to diving in kelp.

Location: About ½ mile (.8km) NW of Pt. Loma, San Diego

Depth Range: 20-50ft (6-15m)

Access: Boat

Expertise Rating: Novice

ANDREW SALLMON

Look for octopuses sleeping in crevices during the day.

South Channel
Shore Dive Sites

In the right place, on the right day, you can have a great beach dive in Southern California. The trick is knowing where to go and when. While many sites have the potential to be great dives, you need to understand how to choose one that is likely to offer decent conditions on a given day.

Geography and weather dominate beach diving conditions. The Southern California Swell Model (http://cdip.ucsd.edu/models/wave.model.shtml), a service

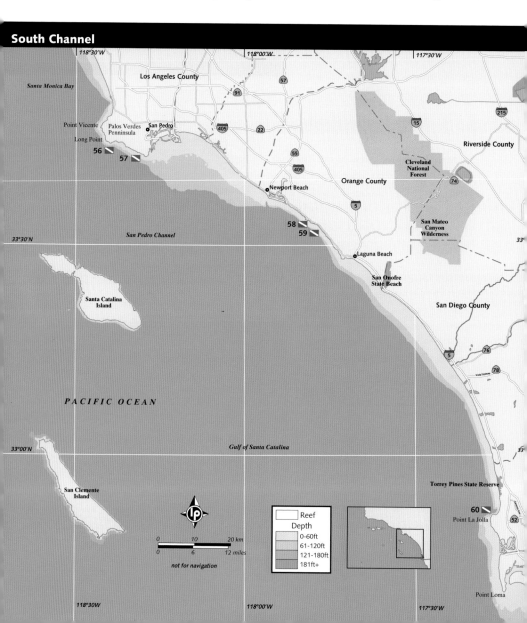

South Channel

of the University of California San Diego, can help you decide where conditions are likely to be favorable. See page 41 for a sample swell model.

From Point Vicente to White Point on the Palos Verdes Peninsula, the coastline runs more or less east and west for about 10 miles (16km). Catalina shelters this area from the south swell. To a lesser degree, Point Conception and Santa Cruz Island shield it from the north.

Catalina partially protects Orange County's beaches from westerly and northerly weather and swells, but they are open to the south. A series of small coves around Laguna Beach—Scotchman's, Fisherman's, Rocky Beach, Moss Street and Wood's Cove—are sometimes less effected by wave action than the surrounding beaches.

In San Diego County the islands are too far offshore and too far north to provide much protection to the shore sites. Sheltered from the south swell by Point La Jolla, a deep inshore trench makes La Jolla Canyon one of the most exciting shore dives in Southern California.

South Channel Shore Dive Sites

	Good Snorkeling	Novice	Intermediate	Advanced
56 Point Vicente	●		●	
57 White Point	●		●	
58 Scotchman's Cove	●		●	
59 Woods Cove & Moss Street	●		●	
60 La Jolla Canyon			●	

56 Point Vicente

About 10 miles wide from east to west, the Palos Verdes Peninsula juts south into the San Pedro Channel. Point Vicente, at the western end of the south-facing side of Palos Verdes, is closer to Catalina's west end than to L.A. City Hall. In the summer, sheltered by Catalina from a moderate south swell, the southern side of Palos Verdes is often calm, clear and warm.

One of a few sites on Palos Verdes open to the public, Point Vicente is less than a mile east (toward San Pedro) of

Location: L.A. County; S face of Palos Verdes Peninsula

Depth Range: 15-40ft (4.6-12m)

Access: Shore

Expertise Rating: Intermediate

the end of Hawthorne Boulevard, a T-junction with Palos Verdes Drive West.

Visit the lighthouse while at Point Vicente.

The free public parking area at the top of the cliff is rarely full. There's a public lavatory with a freshwater tap, but no lifeguard, phone or other facilities.

Point Vicente is an ideal free-diving site. Though the long, winding path is safe to descend in full scuba gear, it's a long haul back up what locals refer to as Cardiac Hill. Just east of Point Vicente, Long Point is easier for those with full dive gear to access, if it's open. The hike from the old Marineland parking lot is not as taxing as the trek at Point Vicente, but the owners often close the site to the public, and the dive can be less interesting.

Point Vicente's rocky beach is the starting point for several interesting sites. Just east of the Point Vicente Lighthouse is a small bay, perhaps three-eighths of a mile wide from east to west. About 100 yards past the western end, directly beneath the lighthouse, a reef marked by kelp and wash rocks extends about 200 yards straight into the channel. It's a long swim, but it's the best dive at Point Vicente. You'll find calico bass, opaleye and yellowtail here. Watch out for boat traffic as you head away from shore.

There's a smaller reef on the eastern end of the bay and some rocks surrounded by sand right in the middle. Occasionally, white sea bass have been known to hang out in these shallows. You may see bat rays and halibut in the sand.

Just west of the lighthouse, the small museum and whale-watching platform are great places to visit after your dive.

Just east of Point Vicente is the Abalone Cove Ecological Reserve. The reserve extends 1 mile west along the coast from Inspiration Point. No invertebrates may be taken out to depths of 20ft.

57 White Point

About a mile west of Point Fermin, near the eastern end of the Palos Verdes Peninsula, White Point usually falls within the swell shadow of Catalina Island. In summer and fall the channel in this area is often dead flat calm, although there may be some current.

White Point Park is at the south end of Western Avenue. For a small fee you can drive down to the beach, park and offload within a few steps of the entry place, a large tide pool known as **Diver's Cove**. The cove is sheltered by rocks on

Location: L.A. County; S face of Palos Verdes Peninsula

Depth Range: 15-40ft (4.6-12m)

Access: Shore

Expertise Rating: Intermediate

all sides. A break in the reef allows access to the outer reef and open water. There's a lifeguard on duty year-round. In the park on top of the hill there are pay phones and a public lavatory.

From the top of the cliff you can easily determine whether it's calm enough to dive. On a calm day you may have 20 to 30ft of vertical visibility underwater. Although you can park within a few yards of the water, traversing the rocky beach in full scuba gear can be a painful experience. It's best to haul your gear to the water wearing your shoes, then gear up.

The reef begins within 50 yards of shore. It runs mostly parallel to the beach for more than a mile in either direction. The outer reef, three-eighths to half a mile from shore, is covered with a vast kelp forest, by far the largest inshore kelp growth in L.A. County. The problem for scuba divers is getting there. The other problem, for all divers, is boat traffic.

White Point is a very fishy place. Especially if you're free-diving, you'll see lots of calico bass, sand bass, opaleye and, in winter (if you're lucky), white sea bass. There are also some natural, hot-water vents very close to shore, near the only break in the reef at the mouth of Diver's Cove. The vents are easy to find because they are marked by mats of white bacterial growth, perhaps a square yard in area and an eighth of an inch thick.

Unimpressive as they may appear, these bacteria are extraordinary lifeforms. Like the *Thiothrix* bacteria found around deep-ocean hydrothermal vents, these subtidal bacteria apparently oxidize sulfur-based compounds rather than carbon-based compounds. Like their deep-ocean relatives, they form the basis of a food chain. According to a study published by Jeffrey L. Stein (*Science Magazine*, February 17, 1984), black abalone and several species of limpets have been observed grazing, and thriving, upon this stuff.

The land on the back side of Palos Verdes was owned by Japanese-American farmers, ab divers and fishermen up until WWII. You can still see bits and pieces of their bathhouse near the geothermal vents.

The Marine Mammal Care Center at Fort McCarthur, the Fort McCarthur Museum, the Korean Bell and the Cabrillo Marine Aquarium are all within a very short distance of White Point.

Look for subtidal bacteria, which oxidize sulfur-based compounds, near the mouth of Diver's Cove.

58 Scotchman's Cove

At the southeast end of Crystal Cove State Park, Scotchman's Cove has several advantages as a shore site: an extensive reef structure, relatively easy entry and exit, plentiful marine life, good facilities (including showers) and lots of parking. You'll find the park along Highway 1 between Corona del Mar and Laguna Beach.

Location: North Orange County; Crystal Cove State Park, S of Newport Beach

Depth Range: 15-50ft (4.6-15m)

Access: Shore

Expertise Rating: Intermediate

BONNIE CARDONE
Colorful macrophoto subjects abound.

The stairway to the dive site is near the restrooms at the top of the hill. The reef, which runs straight out from the shore, is clearly discernible from the stairway. Usually, one side of the reef is calmer than the other. Enter and exit there.

Once known for game fish, Scotchman's Cove is now somewhat "fished out." Still, you can find lobsters in the rocks, as well as calico and sheephead in the kelp. In some places on the outer reefs, the wall drops 20ft or so. In these areas you might find white sea bass in winter. For photographers there are plenty of invertebrate macro subjects on the rocks. Visibility rarely exceeds 30ft.

59 Woods Cove & Moss Street

If you want to dive in Laguna Beach in the summer, arrive early. Woods Cove and Moss Street, adjacent shore sites off Ocean Way in Laguna Beach, are usually less crowded than **Fisherman's Cove, Picnic Beach, Shaw's Cove** and **Rocky Beach**, but the diving is comparable. If you can't park near the intersection of Diamond Street and Ocean Way for access to Woods Cove, try Moss Street, a few blocks farther south on Ocean Way.

There are stairways from the parking areas to the beach at both sites. If you

Location: Orange County; Laguna Beach

Depth Range: 15-40ft (4.6-12m)

Access: Shore

Expertise Rating: Intermediate

want to scuba dive, the climb won't kill you. From the top it's easy to assess conditions. At both sites there's soft sand where you enter and exit. Neither site offers public facilities.

Both sites feature shallow reefs, kelp growth and abundant fish and invertebrates. The most interesting structures at either site (boulders, walls, small caves, overhangs and so forth) begin about 50 yards from the entry near the bottom of the stairway. At Woods Cove there's a large boulder in about 30ft of water that makes boilers perhaps 100 yards from shore. As is usually the case at shore sites, the water clears as you leave the sandy bottom near the shoreline. Don't expect to see more than 30ft in front of you, however.

Look for garibaldi, senorita wrasses, sand bass, calico bass and sheephead. In summer you may see halibut in the sand. Sea fans, small scallops and anemones decorate the rocks. A few lobsters hide in the holes on the outer reefs.

60 La Jolla Canyon

La Jolla Canyon—a spectacular submarine geological feature that extends from miles offshore to within 150 yards of La Jolla Shores Beach—is probably the most exciting shore dive in San Diego County.

Park on Camino del Oro near Vallecitos Street. After an easy entry from the sandy beach, swim on the surface straight out from Lifeguard Station No. 20, which is slightly north of Vallecitos Street. After about 100 yards you'll see a white buoy. Keeping the buoy on your left, take a bearing on the end of Scripp's Pier. Descend when the end of the pier lines up with a green building on the cliff. Exit at Lifeguard Station No. 20.

The bottom falls in a series of walls and ledges to below 200ft. Usually, dozens of bat rays and shovelnose guitarfish sleep on the sandy ledges. Huge schools of baitfish are common, as are large, tame sheephead. Lobsters and octopuses hide in the cracks of the walls.

On spring nights, squid rise from the canyon to spawn. Swimming with the spawning squid is amazing, as bat rays, giant sea bass, leopard sharks and blue sharks converge to feast on squid and squid eggs. Do a daytime dive first, however, to become familiar with the terrain.

Location: San Diego County; La Jolla Shores Beach

Depth Range: 40-130ft (12-40m)

Access: Shore or boat

Expertise Rating: Intermediate

La Jolla Shores and Canyon fall within the La Jolla Underwater Park, as do Goldfish Point and La Jolla Cove (popular and less challenging beach dive sites directly south). Taking, or even disturbing, marine life is forbidden within the reserve. Divers have reported seeing Native American stone pottery in the canyon. These, too, must not be moved.

ANDREW SALLMON
Bat rays sleep on the canyon's sandy ledges.

Marine Life

DAVID MCCRAY

Nourished by cold, deepwater upwellings and stirred by powerful ocean currents, the inshore waters of Southern California provide habitat for thousands of vertebrate and invertebrate species. The plants and animals that populate this marine environment are as beautiful, diverse, abundant and fascinating as those found anywhere else on Earth.

This chapter provides images of animals frequently encountered by divers in Southern California.

The marine life pictured here is identified by its common name, followed by the scientific name (in italics). Common names are used freely but are notoriously inaccurate and inconsistent. The two-part scientific name is more precise. It consists of a genus name followed by a species name. A genus is a group of species that share many common features. A species is a recognizable group of plants or animals that are able to interbreed.

Common Vertebrates

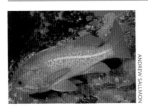

vermilion rockfish
Sebastes miniatus

China rockfish
Sebastes nebulosus

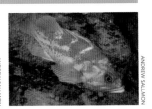

copper rockfish
Sebastes caurinus

black rockfish
Sebastes melanops

treefish
Sebastes serriceps

California moray
Gymnothorax mordax

124

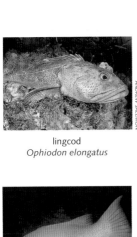

lingcod
Ophiodon elongatus

garibaldi
Hypsypops rubicundus

senorita wrasse
Oxyjulis californica

California sheephead
Semicossyphus pulcher

giant kelpfish
Heterostichus rostratus

blacksmith
Chromis punctipinnis

rubberlip surfperch
Rhacochilus toxotes

California halibut
Paralichthys californicus

leopard shark
Triakis semifasciata

angel shark
Squatina californica

horn shark
Heterodontus francisci

bat ray
Myliobatis californica

Common Invertebrates

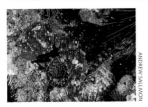

two-spotted octopus
Octopus bimaculatus

California spiny lobster
Panulirus interruptus

sheep crab
Loxorhynchus grandis

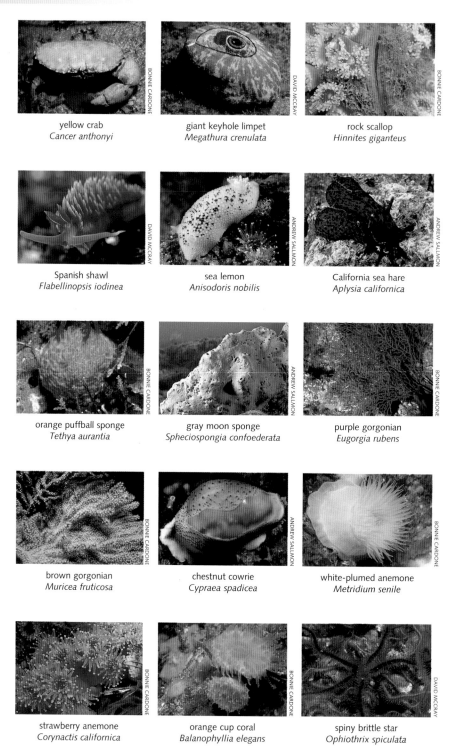

yellow crab
Cancer anthonyi

giant keyhole limpet
Megathura crenulata

rock scallop
Hinnites giganteus

Spanish shawl
Flabellinopsis iodinea

sea lemon
Anisodoris nobilis

California sea hare
Aplysia californica

orange puffball sponge
Tethya aurantia

gray moon sponge
Spheciospongia confoederata

purple gorgonian
Eugorgia rubens

brown gorgonian
Muricea fruticosa

chestnut cowrie
Cypraea spadicea

white-plumed anemone
Metridium senile

strawberry anemone
Corynactis californica

orange cup coral
Balanophyllia elegans

spiny brittle star
Ophiothrix spiculata

Hazardous Marine Life

Marine animals almost never attack divers, but many will deploy formidable defensive or offensive weaponry if threatened, startled or harassed. Conscientious divers learn to recognize potentially hazardous species and to treat them with proper respect. This section displays and discusses some potentially dangerous creatures that divers may encounter in Southern California.

Sea Urchin

Because they graze on kelp holdfasts, sea urchins tend to inhabit shallow, rocky areas. The purple sea urchin (*Strongylocentrotus purpuratus*) and the giant red sea urchin (*Strongylocentrotus franciscanus*) are both common in Southern California. Both have long, sharp spines, capable of penetrating neoprene and skin. If

DAVID MCCRAY

allowed to remain in the wound, broken bits of sea urchin spine can damage surrounding tissue, so it's important to extract them and rinse the wound as soon as possible. If you can't extract a sea urchin spine (especially from an area near a joint) seek medical attention.

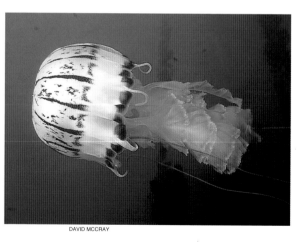

DAVID MCCRAY

Jellyfish

Hundreds of jellyfish species populate Southern California waters. The purple jellyfish (*Pelagia noctiluca*), one of the most common, may reach 1ft (.3m) in diameter with tentacles 6ft (1.8m) long. Stimulated by contact, jellyfish eject barbed stinging cells (called nematocysts) from their tentacles. A diver's wetsuit or gloves usually offer protection when a jellyfish is first touched. Later, however, the

nematocysts may be transferred to bare skin. In most cases, the sting is irritating rather than painful, easily treated with alcohol, vinegar or baking soda. Some people react more adversely than others and may require medical attention.

DAVID MCCRAY

California Scorpionfish

The slow-moving California scorpionfish (*Scorpaena guttata*) relies on excellent camouflage and sharp, poisonous dorsal spines for defense. To avoid an accidental, painful but nonlethal puncture wound, practice good buoyancy control and watch where you put your hands. For first aid, soak the wound in moderately hot water for at least 30 minutes. Cabezon (*Scorpaenichthys marmoratus*) and all rockfish (genus *Sebastes)* also have venomous dorsal spines, but they're not as toxic as scorpionfish.

Electric Ray

Electric rays (*Torpedo californica*) hover in mid-water (often at considerable depth, sometimes under the kelp canopy) or rest on the sand. They are territorial and occasionally aggressive. If one swims right at you, back off. Unique organs generate and store an electrical charge, which the ray discharges to stun prey or repel predators. It won't kill you, but you will sincerely wish you'd left that odd-looking fish alone.

KATHY DEWET-OLESON

Blue Shark

Blue sharks (*Prionace glauca*) cruise near the surface in deep, offshore water. Commonly 6 to 8ft (1.8 to 2.4m) long, they are unafraid of divers, but rarely aggressive. Usually, you have to spread chum in the water to attract them. They feed on squid, mackerel and anchovies, none of which vaguely resembles a diver. However, if

ANDREW SALLMON

excited to feed by chumming or blood from a speared fish, blues can become aggressive. Spearfishing free-divers have reported typical warning-off body language (dropped pectoral fins, arching and twisting) in blue sharks around floating kelp paddies. Encountering a blue shark should not force a diver to exit the water; just monitor the animal's behavior while it remains nearby.

Great White Shark

Obviously, the white shark (*Carcharodon carcharias*) is a potentially dangerous predator. Feeding primarily on pinnipeds, mature individuals reach may reach

20ft (6m) long. Their sharp, serrated teeth and huge, powerful jaws could bite a diver in two. The question is, Do they really pose a significant danger to people in general and divers in particular?

Most researchers believe that white shark attacks occur because the shark has mistaken a person for a prey animal. Great whites hunt sea lions and elephant seals at San Miguel, one of the most popular diving destinations in Southern California. One probably killed a commercial urchin diver there in 1994. Recreational scuba divers, including many spearfishermen, continue to visit San Miguel. Only a handful of scuba divers have reported seeing a great white at San Miguel; none have been attacked. At Catalina, where divers have logged hundreds of thousands of hours, there have been a few white shark encounters in recent years, but no attacks on scuba divers.

It's extremely unlikely, but if you encounter a great white, you should exit the water safely, with all deliberate speed. Because such encounters are so rare, Southern California divers don't worry much about them.

California Cone Shell

This innocent-looking, golden-brown inch-long (2.5cm) mollusk (*Conus californicus*) preys on a greater variety of gastropods than any known cone shell. It kills by inserting an elongated organ beneath the prey animal's shell and injecting a paralyzing, digestive venom. If you pick it up, it may inject that venom into you. It won't kill or digest you, but you will require first aid: vinegar, baking soda, hot water and so forth. If pain or numbness persists, see a doctor.

BONNIE CARDONE

Giant Kelp

Giant kelp (*Macrocystis pyrifera*) presents two problems for divers: in-water entanglement and slippery footing on rocky beaches. You can solve the latter by watching where you're going, or wisely choosing not to do rocky beach entries at low tide.

DAVID MCCRAY

An inexperienced diver entangled in kelp at the surface may start thrashing about, which only makes things worse. Exhausted and low on air, divers have drowned this way. Avoid this by always leaving enough air in your tank to traverse a kelpy area underwater at the end of your dive. If you do get entangled, don't panic. Let your buddy free you by snapping or cutting the kelp strands. It may be a slow process, and a little embarrassing, but it's not life-threatening.

Diving Conservation & Awareness

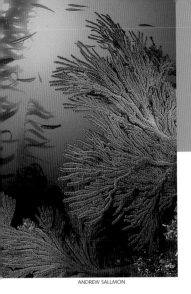

ANDREW SALLMON

In the past half century the rich marine environment of Southern California has been depleted and damaged by commercial fishing, sportfishing, recreational diving, kelp harvesting, industrial and urban pollution, shipping and oil drilling.

San Clemente Island has taken a tremendous pounding as a gunnery target for the U.S. Navy. The Navy also reshaped much of San Nicolas Island, above and below the surface, to suit its needs. On Santa Cruz Island, imported livestock damaged indigenous wildlife and prehistoric archaeological sites.

To curb damage to the marine environment, state and federal agencies regulate marine resource usage, including both commercial and recreational fishing. Be sure to check current Department of Fish and Game regulations before taking anything from Southern California waters (www.dfg.ca.gov/enforcement/regs.html).

The Effects of Sport Diving

Although sport divers harvest less than 1/10,000 of the tonnage taken by commercial fishermen, and though Department of Fish and Game wardens effectively discourage poaching, divers have contributed to the depletion of giant sea bass, hydrocorals, territorial reef fish, scallops and abalone in Southern California waters.

In recent decades many Southern California divers have become active members of organizations like the Santa Catalina Island Conservancy, Heal the Bay and the Giant Sea Bass Project. Still, of all the groups directly affected, recreational divers are underrepresented on the various public commissions that formulate environmental policy.

Since gill netting was banned in the late '80s, sportfishermen and divers have reported a healthy resurgence in the populations of large, pelagic schooling fish like yellowtail and white sea bass. Size and bag limits, as well as seasonal fishery closures, now partially protect several territorial reef fish populations, such as lingcod, rockfish and cabezon. Garibaldi (*Hypsypops rubicundus*), the California state fish, is completely protected in California waters.

The state closed the abalone fishery in Central and Southern California in 1997, following decades of commercial and recreational harvesting and a withering-disease epidemic in the mid-1990s. Of the several species once widespread in Southern California, only red abalone (*Haliotis rufescens*) remain in significant numbers, mostly around San Miguel Island.

California purple hydrocoral once flourished on reefs exposed to nutrient-rich currents. Divers harvested this hydrocoral (*Stylaster californicus*) for use as decorative objects. Now protected, purple hydrocoral is found at Farnsworth Bank (Catalina), Nine Fathom Reef (San Clemente) and at Cortes Bank.

Once common from Baja California to Alaska, California's sea otters (*Enhydra lutris*) were hunted nearly to extinction between 1741 and 1911. Protected by the state since 1913, the southern sea otter population grew from an isolated group of about 50 to about 2,500 animals. By 1990 they ranged from Año Nuevo Point (north of Monterey) to southern San Luis Obispo County, about 50 miles (80km) north of Point Conception and the western end of the Santa Barbara Channel.

Since 1977 the sea otter has been protected under the Federal Endangered Species Act. In an effort to create a satellite population as insurance against the effects of a potential oil spill on the Central Coast, the U.S. Fish & Wildlife Service relocated 140 animals to San Nicolas Island in 1987. By December 1998 only 15 otters remained at San Nicolas. The rest died or swam back to Central California.

Adult sea otters consume up to 15 pounds of abalone, sea urchins, clams, mussels and crabs per day. To protect the commercial shellfish industry, the Fish & Wildlife Service agreed to keep sea otters out of Southern California coastal waters.

In 1998 more than 100 otters migrated south into a mainland cove in Santa Barbara County. Fishermen demanded their removal. The Fish & Wildlife Service, citing the failure of the San Nicolas project, did not remove them. Currently the service is studying new means of protecting the species. For the time being the sea otter has returned to Southern California.

Following oil spills in Huntington Beach, El Segundo and Santa Barbara, environmentalists and fishing industry representatives successfully lobbied congress to establish no-drilling zones in California, partly under the provisions of the National Marine Sanctuaries Acts of 1980 and 1981. Although petroleum companies continue to pump oil from existing offshore wells, exploratory offshore drilling ceased in 1981. According to current law, the moratorium will continue until 2008.

Despite the progress made in recent years, unregulated fishing practices threaten a number of species. The greatest threat to the health of California reef fish populations may be the relatively new and unregulated practice of live-fish trapping. Targeting mostly small rockfish and perch, live-fish trappers place baited devices resembling crab pots on shallow reefs. The trapped fish are sold live to restaurants and seafood markets, particularly in the Asian Pacific.

Sheephead are as yet unprotected, and there is no size limit, although the daily one-species bag limit (10) does apply. Slow and territorial, sheephead have been decimated by spearfishing,

Sheephead have been decimated by spearfishing and live trapping.

DAVID MCCRAY

sportfishing and live trapping. For years divers have reported sparse sheephead populations on mainland coastal reefs. Concerned divers have asked the state to close the sheephead fishery. While the matter is under study, the fate of the sheephead may be decided by the collective conscience of the spearfishing community.

State and federal agencies are under constant and contradictory pressures: to make more public resources available for commercial and industrial development, as well as to further conserve resources. Conservationists and recreational, industrial and commercial interests profoundly disagree on many issues, such as the proposed expansion of no-take zones and the moratorium on oil-drilling in the Channel Islands National Marine Sanctuary.

Harvesting Scallops Responsibly

Taking game from the sea for personal consumption is widely accepted in the Southern California diving community. Most California sport divers harvest game responsibly, but they do tend to revisit the reefs too often. Scallop shells provide habitat for dozens of small invertebrate species. When divers remove scallops, shell and all, they destroy that habitat. There is a way to take scallops that minimizes the destructive consequences to the reef ecosystem.

To harvest scallops, or any other game, you must have a current California Fishing License with an Ocean Enhancement Stamp. Visitors to California may obtain a non-resident fishing license at many dive shops and any marina bait shop.

The daily bag limit for scallops is 10. There is no size limit. Because the currents are rich in plankton, scallops grow large at most Southern California seamounts—2 or 3lb (.9 to 1.5kg) including the shell. To bag the big ones, divers work at depths of 90ft (30m) and more.

With an added 25lbs (11kg) in the bag, a diver may have to kick hard to get off the bottom at such depths. Reaching the surface exhausted and with a depleted tank, he may be too heavy to keep his head above water, even with his BC inflated. Though not far from the boat, he may drown if he is unwilling to dump his game bag or his weight belt. Believe it or not, this has happened.

For safety's sake, some California dive-charter operators ask their patrons to clean scallops on the reef rather than lug them whole to the boat. To clean scallops without dislodging the shell, many experienced divers use a heavy dive knife to wedge the shell open and an abalone (or "ab") iron or a sharp fillet knife to remove the muscular foot.

The ab iron, with its beveled tip, is ideal for scraping the meat from the top side of the shell. Then, with the foot still attached to the bottom side, pull the guts off the meat. Scrape the cleaned meat off the bottom side and pop it into your game bag or BC pocket. It may be slower than grabbing the whole scallop, but it's actually easier than trying to open and clean a snapped-tight scallop topside. Cleaning scallops on the reef is safer, provides no amusement to other divers and does far less damage to the reef.

BONNIE CARDONE

Marine Reserves & Regulations

Channel Islands National Marine Sanctuary

Established in 1980, the Channel Islands National Marine Sanctuary is a protected marine environment administered by the National Oceanic and Atmospheric Administration (NOAA), a branch of the Department of Commerce. Its boundaries extend from mean high tide to six nautical miles (11.4km) offshore of each of the four North Channel Islands (San Miguel, Santa Rosa, Santa Cruz and Anacapa) and Santa Barbara Island. The Channel Islands National Park includes the islands as well as the waters surrounding them to a distance of one nautical mile. Certain activities are restricted or prohibited within the sanctuary: dumping of waste materials, drilling through the seabed, operating a commercial vessel within 1 mile (1.6km) of the islands (with the exception of fishing, kelp harvesting, recreational or research vessels), flying a plane at less than 1,000ft (300m) above sea level, and removing or damaging shipwrecks or archaeological artifacts.

Originally mandated to protect ocean wilderness areas primarily against the effects of oil drilling and waste dumping, the Marine Sanctuary System now seeks to expand its authority to protect fish and wildlife within its boundaries. The establishment of no-take zones is currently under study.

Offshore Rocks & Pinnacles Ecological Reserve

Also called the California Coastal National Monument, this reserve protects wildlife on federally owned exposed reefs, rocks and pinnacles within 12 miles (19.2km) of shore. These land formations provide haul-out space for pinnipeds and nesting habitat for about 200,000 seabirds.

Reserves & Refuges

There are more than 20 reserves, ecological reserves and marine life refuges in Southern California, each with its own set of protective prohibitions and restrictions. In general, reserves and ecological reserves protect some or all marine species within their boundaries. Marine life refuges prohibit or at least restrict commercial fishing and, less often, sportfishing. Many dive sites are either completely or partially within (or in some cases, very close to) the following protected areas:

San Miguel Island Ecological Reserve
Santa Barbara Island Ecological Reserve
East Anacapa Island Natural Area & Ecological Reserve
Anacapa Island Ecological Reserve
Avalon Underwater Park, Catalina Island
Lover's Cove Reserve, Catalina Island
Catalina Marine Science Center Marine Life Refuge, Catalina Island
Farnsworth Ecological Reserve, Catalina Island
Abalone Cove Ecological Reserve
La Jolla Ecological Reserve

Responsible Diving

Dive sites tend to be located where the reefs and walls display the most beautiful marine life. By following certain basic guidelines while diving, you can help preserve the ecology and beauty of the reefs:

1. Practice and maintain proper buoyancy control and avoid over-weighting. Be aware that buoyancy can change over the period of an extended trip. Initially you may breathe harder and need more weighting; a few days later you may breathe more easily and need less weight. Tip: Use your weight belt and tank position to maintain a horizontal position—raise them to elevate your feet, lower them to elevate your upper body. Also be careful about buoyancy loss: As you go deeper, your wetsuit compresses, as does the air in your BC.

2. Avoid touching living marine organisms with your body and equipment. Though holding on to the mostly granite substrate normally doesn't do much damage, choose handholds carefully to avoid harming marine life.

3. Take great care in underwater caves, ledges and other tight areas. The heavy surge can be dangerous, throwing you into the rocks and walls. Divers should take turns inspecting these areas to lessen the danger.

4. Secure gauges, computer consoles and the octopus regulator so they're not dangling—they are like miniature wrecking balls to a reef and can become entangled in the kelp.

5. When swimming in strong currents, be extra careful about leg kicks and handholds.

6. Photographers should take extra precautions as cameras and equipment affect buoyancy. Changing f-stops, framing a subject and maintaining position for a photo often conspire to prohibit the ideal "no-touch" approach. When you must use "holdfasts," choose them intelligently.

7. Resist the temptation to collect or buy marine-life souvenirs. Aside from the ecological damage, taking home marine souvenirs depletes the beauty of a site and spoils other divers' enjoyment.

8. Ensure that you take home all your trash. Plastics in particular pose a serious threat to marine life.

9. Resist the temptation to feed fish. You may disturb their normal eating habits, encourage aggressive behavior or feed them food that is detrimental to their health.

10. Minimize your disturbance of marine animals. Enforced by the National Marine Fisheries Service, the Marine Mammal Protection Act of 1972 stipulates that marine mammals (such as sea otters, whales, seals and sea lions) may not be hunted, harassed, captured or killed and provides for the establishment of marine mammal rescue and rehabilitation centers. Divers must understand that initiating contact with a marine mammal could be interpreted as harassment.

Listings

Telephone Calls

If you are calling within the U.S., dial 1 + the area code + the local 7-digit number. Toll-free (800 or 888) numbers can be accessed from the U.S. and, usually, Canada.

Accommodations & Other Information

Accommodations information, maps, brochures and tickets to theme parks and other attractions are available through convention and visitors bureaus, tourist offices and chambers of commerce operated by many of Southern California's cities and counties. (Be aware that chambers of commerce tend to have an interest in promoting their members first, and therefore aren't necessarily objective.) Contact any of these agencies for specific information about accommodations or attractions within its jurisdiction:

Anaheim/Orange County
☎ 714-999-8999

Catalina Island Chamber of Commerce
☎ 310-510-1520
www.visitcatalina.com

Hermosa Beach Chamber of Commerce
☎ 310-376-0951
www.hbchamber.net

Long Beach Convention & Visitors Bureau
Toll-free ☎ 800-452-7829
www.golongbeach.org

Los Angeles Convention & Visitors Bureau
☎ 213-689-8822
www.lacvb.com

Malibu Chamber of Commerce
☎ 310-456-9025
www.malibu.org

Marina del Rey Chamber of Commerce
☎ 310-645-5151
www.wlaxmdrchamber.com

San Pedro Peninsula Chamber of Commerce
☎ 310-832-7272
www.sanpedrochamber.com

Santa Monica Convention & Visitors Bureau
☎ 310-319-6263
www.santamonica.com

Venice Area Chamber of Commerce
☎ 310-396-7016
www.venice.net

State & National Parks

California State Parks
Toll-free ☎ 800-444-PARK
www.cal-parks.ca.gov
CSP Angeles District
☎ 818-880-0350
CSP Channel Coast District
☎ 805-899-1400
CSP Orange Coast District
☎ 949-492-0802
CSP San Diego Coast District
☎ 858-642-4200

Channel Islands National Park
1901 Spinnaker Dr.
Ventura, CA 93001
☎ 805-658-5730
www.channel.islands
.national-park.com
www.nps.gov

Crystal Cove State Park
Pacific Coast Highway,
S. Orange County
☎ 949-494-3539

Gaviota State Park
Highway 101, N. Santa Barbara County
☎ 805-968-1033

Leo Carrillo State Beach
Pacific Coast Highway,
N. L.A. County
☎ 818-880-0350

Point Mugu State Park
Pacific Coast Highway,
S. Ventura County
☎ 818-880-0350

State & National Parks (continued)

Refugio State Beach
Highway 101, N. Santa Barbara
County
☎ 805-968-1033

San Clemente State Beach
Off I-5, S. Orange County
☎ 949-492-3156

San Onofre State Beach
Off I-5, N. San Diego County
☎ 949-492-4872

Diving Services

The following dive shops, equipment retailers, custom wetsuit manufacturers or diving specialty service shops are no more than 15 miles from a major harbor or beach dive site. They offer a range of rental and retail gear, airfills and certification classes. All facilities offering instruction should display their appropriate affiliations (NAUI, PADI, SSI, etc.). Most major credit cards are accepted.

Santa Barbara County

Anacapa Dive Center
22 Anacapa St.
Santa Barbara, CA 93101
☎ 805-963-8917

Aquatics
5708 Hollister Ave.
Goleta, CA 93117
☎ 805-967-4456

California Watersports
5822 Hollister Ave.

Santa Barbara, CA 93117
☎ 805-964-0180

Deep Thought
5708 Hollister Ave.
Goleta, CA 93117
☎ 805-681-2515

**Diving Equipment Co.
of America**
333 E. Haley St.

Santa Barbara, CA 93101
☎ 805-564-1923

Diving Systems International
425 Garden St.
Santa Barbara, CA 93101
☎ 805-965-8538

Harbor Watersports Center
117 Harbor Way
Santa Barbara, CA 93109
☎ 805-962-4890

Ventura County

Aqua-Ventures Inc.
2172 Pickwick Dr.
Camarillo, CA 93010
☎ 805-484-1594

Channel Islands Scuba
4255 E. Main
Ventura, CA 93003
☎ 805-644-3483

Kayak Diving
843 Via Montanez

Camarillo, CA 93012
☎ 805-384-0124

Le Grand Bleu
2055 Harbor Blvd.
Ventura, CA 93001
☎ 805-652-1199

Pacific Scuba Center Inc.
3600 Harbor Blvd.
Oxnard, CA 93035
☎ 805-984-2566

Sport Chalet
1885 E. Ventura Blvd.
Oxnard, CA 93030
☎ 805-485-5222

Tanks Unlimited
4464 McGrath St.
Ventura, CA 93003
☎ 805-658-1561

Ventura Dive & Sport
1559 Spinnaker Dr.
Ventura, CA 93001
☎ 805-650-6595

Los Angeles County

American Diving
1901 Pacific Coast Highway
Lomita, CA 90717
☎ 310-326-6663

**Blue Cheer Dive & Surf
Center**
1110 Wilshire Blvd.
Santa Monica, CA 90401
☎ 310-319-1370

Divers' Discount.Com
9197 Central Ave. H
Montclair, CA 91763 or
3575 Cahuenga Blvd. W. #104
Los Angeles, CA 90068
Toll-free ☎ 800-347-2822

Dive N' Surf Inc.
504 N. Broadway

Redondo Beach, CA 90277
☎ 310-372-8423

JMJ Wetsuits
2331 Abalone Ave.
Torrance, CA 90501
☎ 310-212-3040

Los Angeles County (continued)

Malibu Divers
21231 W. Pacific Coast
Highway
Malibu, CA 90265
☎ 310-456-2396

Ocean Adventures Dive Co.
1915 Lincoln Blvd.
Venice, CA 90291
☎ 310-578-9391

M & B Wet Suit Design
4414 E. Village Road
Long Beach, CA 90808
☎ 562-421-9905

New England Divers Inc.
2936 Clark Ave.
Long Beach, CA 90815
☎ 562-421-8939

**Pacific Sporting Goods
Scuba Center**
11 39th Place
Long Beach, CA 90803
☎ 562-434-1604

Pacific Wilderness
1719 S. Pacific Ave.
San Pedro, CA 90731
☎ 310-833-2422

Santa Monica Water Sports
2204½ Pico Blvd.
Santa Monica, CA 90405
☎ 310-581-2717

Sea D Sea
1911 S. Catalina Ave.
Redondo Beach, CA 90277
☎ 310-373-6355

Splash Dive Co.
2490 Lincoln Blvd.
Venice, CA 90291
Toll-free ☎ 800-997-2822

Sport Chalet
7440 Carson Blvd.
Long Beach, CA 90808
☎ 562-429-9560

Sport Chalet
100 N. La Cienega Blvd.
Los Angeles, CA 90048
☎ 310-657-3210

Sport Chalet
13455 Maxella Ave.
Marina Del Rey, CA 90292
☎ 310-821-9400

Catalina Island

Catalina Divers Supply
Pleasure Pier
Avalon, CA 90704
☎ 310-510-0330

Catalina Scuba Luv
126 Catalina Ave.
Avalon, CA 90704
☎ 310-510-2350

Orange County

**A-1 Stop Non-Stop Scuba
Training & Repair Center**
1800 E. 1st St.
Santa Ana, CA 92705
☎ 714-835-5544

Adventures in Diving
31676 S. Coast Highway
Laguna Beach, CA 92651
☎ 949-499-4517

Aquatic Center
4537 W. Coast Highway
Newport Beach, CA 92663
☎ 949-650-5440

Beach Cities Scuba Mania
19036 Brookhurst St.
Huntington Beach, CA 92646
☎ 714-378-2611

Bottom Time Scuba
1925 Harbor Blvd.
Costa Mesa, CA 92627
☎ 949-645-3483

Divegear Inc.
1280 Bison B9255
Newport Beach, CA 92660
☎ 949-644-4930

Divers' Discount.Com
30308 Esperanza
Rancho Santa Margarita,
CA 92688
☎ 949-459-9400

Laguna Sea Sports
925 N. Coast Highway
Laguna Beach, CA 92651
☎ 949-494-6965

Laguna Surf & Sport Inc.
1088 S. Coast Highway
Laguna Beach, CA 92651
☎ 949-497-7000

Liburdis Scuba Center Inc.
15315 Culver Dr.
Irvine, CA 92604
☎ 949-857-6722

**National Scuba Repair
& Hydro**
17551 Gothard St.
Huntington Beach, CA 92647
☎ 714-847-4386

Openwater Habitat
1800 E. 1st St.
Santa Ana, CA 92705
☎ 714-646-7111

Pacific Discount Dive Sales
P.O. Box 3561
Dana Point, CA 92629
☎ 949-831-7222

Scubatech
1668 Babcock St.
Costa Mesa, CA 92627
☎ 949-650-5922

Sea Stallion Scuba Outfitters
16 Technology Dr.
Irvine, CA 92618
☎ 949-450-0404

Sport Chalet
27080 Alicia Parkway
Laguna Niguel, CA 92677
☎ 949-362-0342

Sport Chalet
16242 Beach Blvd.
Huntington Beach, CA 92647
☎ 714-848-0988

Sport Chalet
2983 Michelson Dr.
Irvine, CA 92612
☎ 949-476-9555

Orange County (continued)

Victory Wetsuits
15811 Graham St.
Huntington Beach, CA 92649
☎ 714-894-0621

500 PSI
35381 Camino Capistrano
Capistrano Beach, CA 92624
☎ 949-248-4818

San Diego County

Aqua Tech Dive Center
1800 Logan Ave.
San Diego, CA 92113
☎ 619-237-1800

Blue Escape
1617 Quivira Rd.
San Diego, CA 92109
☎ 619-223-3483

Breeze Flow Wetsuits
602 Mission Ave.
Oceanside, CA 92054
☎ 760-722-5803

Diving Locker
1020 Grand Ave.
San Diego, CA 92109
☎ 858-272-1120

North County Scuba Center
122 Encinitas Blvd.
Encinitas, CA 92024
☎ 760-753-0036

OE Express
2158 Avenida de la Playa
La Jolla, CA 92037
☎ 858-454-6195

Pyramid Divers Inc.
282 Harbor Dr. South
Oceanside, CA 92054
☎ 760-433-6842

**San Diego Divers Supply
Discount Outlet**
4004 Sports Arena Blvd.
San Diego, CA 92110
☎ 619-224-3439

Scuba San Diego
1775 E. Mission Bay Dr.
San Diego, CA 92116
☎ 619-260-1880

Scuba San Diego Get Wet
4122 Napier St.
San Diego, CA 92110
☎ 619-275-3483

Sea Me Repair
4352 Poplar St.
San Diego, CA 92105
☎ 619-563-9033

Sport Chalet
3695 Midway Dr.
San Diego, CA 92110
☎ 619-224-6777

Sport Chalet
1640 Camino Del Rio North
San Diego, CA 92108
☎ 619-718-7070

Sport Chalet
4545 La Jolla Village Dr.
San Diego, CA 92122
☎ 858-453-5656

Surf 'N Sea Custom Wet Suits
1874 Bacon St.
San Diego, CA 92107
☎ 619-222-1231

Dive Boat Operations

This list, arranged alphabetically by home port, includes most of the full-time dive charter boats operating in Southern California at the time of publication. For a complete current list, log on to The Scuba Divers Network at www.diver.net. For a nearly complete current schedule see *California Diving News*.

The number of divers refers to the maximum diver load on one-day trips. The limit for multi-day trips is always less. All boats offering multi-day (live-aboard) trips provide bunks and full galley service.

Truth Aquatics
301 W. Cabrillo Rd., Santa Barbara, CA 93101
☎ 805-962-1127, www.truthaquatics.com
Conception: 78ft boat, 40 divers, 3,000 psi fills,
E6 photo processing, one-day & multi-day trips
Truth: 65ft boat, 32 divers, 3,000 psi fills,
one-day & multi-day trips
Vision: 80ft boat, 40 divers, 3,000 psi fills, E6
photo processing, one-day & multi-day trips
Home Port: Santa Barbara
Destinations: San Miguel, Santa Rosa, Santa Cruz
& Anacapa Islands, Santa Barbara Channel oil rigs

Liberty
1567 Spinnaker Dr., #203-59, Ventura, CA 93001
☎ 805-642-6655, divliberty@aol.com
75ft boat, 40 divers, 3,000 psi fills, hot tub,
one-day trips
Home Port: Ventura
Destinations: Anacapa & Santa Cruz Islands,
Santa Barbara Channel oil rigs

Peace
1567 Spinnaker Dr., #203-393, Ventura,
CA 93001
☎ 805-984-2025, www.peaceboat.com

65ft boat, 32 divers, 3,500 psi fills, nitrox on board, camera charging station, hot tub, one-day & multi-day trips
Home Port: Ventura
Destinations: San Miguel, Santa Rosa, Santa Cruz, Anacapa, Santa Barbara, San Nicolas & San Clemente Islands, Cortes & Tanner Banks, Santa Barbara Channel oil rigs

Spectre
1567 Spinnaker Dr. #203-59, Ventura, CA 93001
☎ 805-483-6612, www.takemetoo.com
85ft boat, 40 divers, 3,000 psi fills, one-day trips
Home Port: Ventura
Destinations: Anacapa & Santa Cruz Islands

Great Escape Charters
P.O. Box 14773, Long Beach, CA 90853
☎ 562-983-5626, www.diveboat.com
Great Escape: 80ft boat, 35 divers, 3,200 psi fills, camera charging station, one-day & multi-day trips
Home Port: San Pedro
Destinations: Santa Catalina, San Clemente, Santa Barbara & San Nicolas Islands, Cortes & Tanner Banks

Westerly
141 22nd St., San Pedro, CA 90731
☎ 310-850-8186
55ft boat, 26 divers, 2,500 psi fills, mostly one-day trips
Home Port: San Pedro
Destinations: Santa Catalina, Santa Barbara & San Clemente Islands

Bottom Scratcher Charters
555 Pico Ave., Long Beach, CA 90802
☎ 714-963-4378, www.bottomscratcher.com
Bottom Scratcher: 63ft boat, 30 divers, 3,700 psi fills, tanks & weights supplied, one-day & multi-day trips
Home Port: Long Beach
Destinations: Santa Catalina, San Clemente, Santa Barbara & San Nicolas Islands

Charisma Charter Service
P.O. Box 590, Harbor City, CA 90710
☎ 310-541-1025, diveboat@msn.com
Encore: 80ft boat, 36 divers, 3,000 psi fills, one-day & multi-day trips
Home Port: Long Beach
Destinations: Santa Catalina, San Clemente, Santa Barbara & San Nicolas Islands, Cortes & Tanner Banks

Diving Charters Inc.
P.O. Box 2496, Corona, CA 92878
☎ 909-279-3483, www.diving.net
Sand Dollar: 65ft boat, 32 divers, 2,400 psi fills, nitrox on board, one-day & multi-day trips
Home Port: Long Beach
Destinations: Santa Catalina, San Clemente, Santa Barbara & San Nicolas Islands

Catalina Divers Supply Charters
P.O. Box 126, Avalon, CA 90704
Toll-free ☎ 800-353-0330,
www.diveinfo.com/cds/index.html
Scuba Cat: 46ft boat, 24 divers, no fills, snacks, tanks & weights supplied, mostly half-day trips
Home Port: Avalon
Destinations: Santa Catalina Island

Catalina Scuba Luv
P.O. Box 2009, Avalon, CA 90704
Toll-free ☎ 800-262-3483, prneptune@aol.com
King Neptune: 65ft boat, 30 divers, 3,500 psi fills, full galley, tanks & weights supplied, nitrox available (no refills), two-tank & three-tank trips
Prince Neptune: 33ft boat, 6 divers, no fills, continental breakfast & deli lunch, tanks & weights supplied, guided dive, nitrox available (no refills), two-tank & three-tank trips
Home Port: Avalon
Destinations: Santa Catalina Island, shark-cage diving

Blue Escape Dive & Charter Inc.
1617 Quivira Rd., Suite B, San Diego, CA 92109
Toll-free ☎ 888-500-3483, www.blueescape.com
Blue Escape: 50ft boat, 22 divers, 3,500 psi fills, nitrox available (no refills), tanks & weights supplied, half-day & full-day trips
Home Port: San Diego
Destinations: Wreck Alley, inshore kelp beds, Coronado Islands

Horizon Charters
2803 Emerson St., San Diego, CA 92106
☎ 858-277-7823, www.horizoncharters.com
Horizon: 80ft boat, 36 divers, 3,300 psi fills, one-day & multi-day trips
Home Port: San Diego
Destinations: San Clemente, San Nicolas, Santa Catalina and Santa Barbara Islands, Cortes & Tanner Banks, Guadalupe Island (Mex.), San Martin Island (Mex.), San Benito Islands (Mex.)

Lois Ann Dive Charters
2803 Emerson St., San Diego, CA 92106
Toll-free ☎ 800-201-4381, www.loisann.com
Lois Ann: 47ft boat, 20 divers, 4,000 psi fills, nitrox on board, tanks & weights supplied, half-day & one-day trips
Home Port: San Diego
Destinations: Wreck Alley, inshore kelp beds, Coronado Islands

Dive Connections Inc.
1845 Quivira Rd., San Diego, CA 92109
Toll-free ☎ 888-420-3047, www.gottadive.com
One Eyed Jack: 32ft boat, 18 divers, no fills, hot lunch, tanks & weights supplied, half-day & one-day trips
Home Port: San Diego
Destinations: Wreck Alley, inshore kelp beds, Coronado Islands, shark-cage dive

Underwater Photography & Video

A B C Photo
9136 S. Sepulveda Blvd.
Los Angeles, CA 90045
☎ 310-645-8992

Los Angeles Underwater
Photographic Society
P.O. Box 2401
Culver City, California
☎ 310-452-0345
info@laups.net

San Diego Underwater
Photographic Society
P.O. Box 82782
San Diego, CA 92138
☎ 877-425-9256

Marine Conservation Organizations

California Artificial Reef
Enhancement Program
Toll-free ☎ 800-804-6002
www.calreefs.org

Santa Catalina Island
Conservancy
☎ 310-510-1421
www.catalinaconservancy.org

Catalina Conservancy Divers
☎ 310-510-2595
www.ccd.org

Earthjustice
www.earthjustice.org

Friends of the Sea Lion
Marine Mammal Center
☎ 949-494-3050
www.fslmmc.org

Heal the Bay
☎ 310-453-0395
Toll-free ☎ 800-HEAL-BAY (in
California only)
www.healthebay.org

National Marine Fisheries
Service
www.nmfs.noaa.gov

The Nature Conservancy
☎ 805-962-9111
www.tnc.org

Santa Barbara Marine
Mammal Center
☎ 805-964-0905

SeaWorld California
Toll-free ☎ 800-541-SEAL
www.seaworld.org/
AnimalRescue

Surfrider Foundation USA
☎ 949-492-8170
www.surfrider.org

Other Resources

The Catalina Express
Ports of Call, San Pedro
Long Beach Harbor
Dana Point Marina
Avalon & Two Harbors, Santa
Catalina Island
Toll-free ☎ 800-481-3470
www.catalinaexpress.com

Channel Islands Aviation
Camarillo Airport
305 Durley Ave.
Camarillo, CA 93010
☎ 805-987-1301
www.flycia.com

Handicapped Scuba
Association International
1104 El Prado

San Clemente, CA 92672
☎ 949-498-6128
www.hsascuba.com

Island Packers
1867 Spinnaker Dr.
Ventura, CA 93001
☎ 805-642-1393
or ☎ 805-382-1779
www.islandpackers.com

Useful Websites

California Department of Fish and Game
www.dfg.ca.gov/dfghome.html

California Diving News
www.saintbrendan.com

California Dive Club List
www.deepdiversions.com/scuba/clublist
.htm# CALIFORNIA

Divers Alert Network
www.diversalertnetwork.org

National Weather Service Los Angeles Area
Marine Weather Page
www.nwsla.noaa.gov/marine.html

Scuba Divers Network
www.diver.net

Southern California Swell Model
http://cdip.ucsd.edu/models/wave.model.shtml

Terry Maas' Free-Diving Page
www.freedive.net

Index

dive sites covered in this book appear in **bold** type

Lonely Planet Pisces Books

The **Diving & Snorkeling** guides cover top destinations worldwide. Beautifully illustrated with full-color photos throughout, the series explores the best diving and snorkeling areas and prepares divers for what to expect when they get there. Each site is described in detail, with information on suggested ability levels, depth, visibility and, of course, marine life. There's basic topside information as well for each destination.

Also check out dive guides to:

Australia: Southeast Coast	Cocos Island	Jamaica	Texas
Bali & Lombok	Cuba	Pacific Northwest	Thailand
Bermuda	Curaçao	Puerto Rico	Trinidad & Tobago
Bonaire	Dominica	Red Sea	Turks & Caicos
British Virgin Islands	Florida Keys	Scotland	Vanuatu
Cayman Islands	Guam & Yap	Seychelles	